DANCE UNITS FOR MIDDLE SCHOOL

Judi Fey

JEROME LIBRARY
CURRICULUM RESOURCE CENTER
BOWLING GREEN STATE UNIVERSITY
BOWLING GREEN, OHIO 43403

Human Kinetics

Library of Congress Cataloging-in-Publication Data

Fey, Judi.
   Dance units for middle school / Judi Fey.
      p. cm.
   Includes bibliographical references.
   ISBN-13: 978-0-7360-8367-6 (soft cover)
   ISBN-10: 0-7360-8367-7 (soft cover)
   1. Dance--Study and teaching (Middle school)--United States. 2. Dance--Study and teaching
(Secondary)--United States. 3. Dance--Curricula--United States. I. Title.
   GV1589.G49 2010
   793.307--dc22

                                            2010020292

ISBN-10: 0-7360-8367-7 (print)
ISBN-13: 978-0-7360-8367-6 (print)

The Web addresses cited in this text were current as of May 2010, unless otherwise noted.

Acquisitions Editors: Judy Patterson Wright, PhD, and Gayle Kassing, PhD; **Developmental Editor:** Jacqueline Eaton Blakley; **Assistant Editor:** Anne Rumery; **Copyeditor:** Jan Feeney; **Graphic Designer:** Fred Starbird; **Graphic Artist:** Yvonne Griffith; **Cover Designer:** Keith Blomberg; **CD and DVD Face Designer:** Susan Rothermel Allen; **Photographer (cover and interior):** Scott Swanson; **Art Manager:** Kelly Hendren; **Associate Art Manager and Illustrator:** Alan L. Wilborn; **Printer:** Versa Press

Printed in the United States of America   10 9 8 7 6 5 4 3 2 1

The paper in this book is certified under a sustainable forestry program.

Human Kinetics
Web site: www.HumanKinetics.com

United States: Human Kinetics
P.O. Box 5076
Champaign, IL 61825-5076
800-747-4457
e-mail: humank@hkusa.com

Canada: Human Kinetics
475 Devonshire Road Unit 100
Windsor, ON N8Y 2L5
800-465-7301 (in Canada only)
e-mail: info@hkcanada.com

Europe: Human Kinetics
107 Bradford Road
Stanningley
Leeds LS28 6AT, United Kingdom
+44 (0) 113 255 5665
e-mail: hk@hkeurope.com

Australia: Human Kinetics
57A Price Avenue
Lower Mitcham, South Australia 5062
08 8372 0999
e-mail: info@hkaustralia.com

New Zealand: Human Kinetics
P.O. Box 80
Torrens Park, South Australia 5062
0800 222 062
e-mail: info@hknewzealand.com

E4845

CONTENTS

UNIT ONE   1
IMPROVISATION

UNIT TWO   45
DANCE FOR ATHLETES

UNIT THREE   89
JAZZ DANCE

PREFACE

As research continues to confirm the link between participation in the arts and academic achievement, more school systems are adding dance to the middle school experience. However, hiring a full-time dance education–certified teacher may not be in the budget initially or at all. Therefore, volunteers in the form of physical educators, faculty members with an interest in dance, teachers' aides, or any other staff members may be tasked with teaching dance. This book, DVD, and CD package has been created for just such volunteers. Conceptualized by physical educators who are also dance trained, this resource offers step-by-step help to middle school physical educators (or other non-dance-trained or certified staff members) charged with teaching middle school dance.

WHY TEACH DANCE?

There are so many reasons why dance is an excellent educational tool. Understanding the history of dance helps students broaden their view of the world. Dance has a rich history that began with the rudiments of cave men and women and continues to evolve today. Early dances were created for specific purposes—to ask for successful crops or fertility, to celebrate, to entertain, and to compete with other villages and prove physical prowess. Dance was a vital part of community identity. As societies became more sophisticated, refinements occurred, such as costumes, makeup, steps with names, and specific dances that were passed down through generations. Dance teachers came about and were held in high regard. In European courts, dancers wearing elaborate costumes and men performing strenuous dances were A-list events. As people traveled and communicated, ideas were shared and new dances were created. People trained to become professional dancers while others danced for recreation and pleasure. Classical dance steps were developed and named in French. Costumes changed to allow less-restricted movement, and women were partnered and lifted by men. Choreographers created elaborate story ballets (fairy-tale types) and set them for dance companies. Before videos, choreographers wrote down their choreography so that others could re-create it. Dancers rebelled, decided there were other ways to dance besides classically, and used dance to make social and political statements. That was the genesis of modern dance. Gayle Kassing's book *History of Dance* (Human Kinetics, 2007) is a wonderful resource for the dance lessons in this book and can provide ideas for enrichment for students interested in history as well as ideas for lessons in partnering dance and other subject areas.

Today we have ballet (classical and contemporary), many modern dance styles, ballroom dance, preserved folk dances, jazz dance, theatrical dance, tap dance, dances from many cultures, fitness dance, and much more. We have so many music styles to which we can dance. The choices are endless, and everyone from novices to trained professionals can enjoy dancing at any level. Thanks to the current plethora of dance shows, people have been introduced to many forms of dance. It is obvious that more and more people understand what they are seeing and appreciate it. This has encouraged people to dance, and students and parents are asking for dance classes as part of the academic school day as a result. The interest is there!

There is no longer any doubt that regular participation in the arts means better academic achievement. Years of research have demonstrated this relationship—notably, *Critical Links,* a compilation sponsored by the Arts Education Partnership and National Endowment for the Arts, and the research of the National Dance Education Organization (NDEO, www.ndeo.org). One reason for this link might be that the knowledge, creativity, and analytical skill required for creating dance are the same that are required for success in academic subjects and life in general. For instance, dance has a specific relationship to mathematics in that it involves numerical patterns, geometric shapes, and planes. Mastery of scientific concepts such as levels, gravity, force, motion, and giving and taking weight are critical to dancing economically. (Brigham Young University teaches physics in the dance studio!) Dance has its own vocabulary; students learn to communicate with another language. Dance processes, such as choreography and aesthetic criticism, foster higher-level learning skills. Further, brain research shows the link between movement and academic learning and the maintenance of brain ability throughout life.

Beyond being linked to academic success, movement and physical fitness are a critical aspect of students' education, just as movement and physical fitness are a critical aspect of a healthy and well-balanced life. Dance certainly contributes to the health-related components of physical fitness: cardiorespiratory conditioning, muscular strength, muscular endurance, flexibility, and body composition. A healthy student should have a healthy body mass index (BMI), be able to walk or run a mile at a pace that keeps the heart strong, have the strength to perform routine tasks and keep the muscles strong, have the muscular endurance to perform tasks and to survive, and maintain range of motion in the joints in order to move easily and prevent injury. Most physical education programs assess these components regularly to help students and parents understand current levels of fitness and how to achieve healthier levels, if necessary. While testing is not part of the dance units in this book, it certainly could be an add-on. Various tests and the software for analysis are available (e.g., from the Physical Best Web site at www.aahperd.org/naspe/professionaldevelopment/physicalBest/).

Dance also improves the skill-related components of physical fitness: agility, balance, coordination, power, reaction time, and speed. In Anne Arundel County Public Schools in Maryland, a high school course called Dance for Athletes has existed for many years. Teacher Melissa Quigley did research that showed the positive change in fitness components of the athletes by the end of the semester. The article "The Impact of Dance on High School Athletes' Agility and Flexibility," authored by Quigley and Joella Mehrhof, was published in the *KAPHERD Journal* (see resource list). Unit II in this book, Dance for Athletes, encourages athletes to use dance training to enhance their athletic performance (cross-training).

Dance provides movement opportunities for many people who find other forms of activity uninviting. It reaches many students who do not enjoy sports or competition, so it can be a great way to involve a wider range of students in physical activity. These units encourage students to make dance their form of lifetime fitness. Dance is also a fitness enhancement for students involved in sports or other forms of movement. A body trained in a variety of ways and able to move economically and comfortably is less likely to be injured and more likely to continue moving throughout life. The dance units in this book can be as athletic as the students make them. They can also be as creative as the students make them. Students can compete in their projects—or not. Athletes perform on the field. The dance units give students performance opportunities as well.

Learning dance can be particularly enjoyable for middle school students. They love their music, and moving to music is motivation for many who are not interested in silent forms of exercise. Moving to music and a rhythm simply feels good. Moving to music of various tempos challenges body control. Moving to music of various moods allows people to put feelings and energy into the movement. Moving to music helps get rid of stress.

Some students simply are not competitive. Dance is a hook for getting them to move without being concerned about who is doing better or whose score is higher. It's an opportunity for students to be themselves and enjoy creating movement without any right or wrong conditions. It is an opportunity to work with others without competing with them.

For social students, working with others to create something or to make a statement allows for social energy to be put to a constructive purpose. It also helps students learn to communicate verbally with others and compromise to have a successful group effort. The student-created dance projects in the units promote this skill. There is growing concern that students spend too much time communicating electronically (such as with texting or computer social network sites), and the projects in this book will help students in their face-to-face communication skills.

Dance is fun and sometimes funny. There is time for humor. There is time to play with movement. There is time to understand that working toward perfecting skills is fun and that working with a group to create something the group is proud of is also fun. Students who have been taught these units have learned a lot about themselves and their ability and creativity, have had experiences completely different than what they are used to, and can hardly wait for the next dance unit. They also wanted more time to work on their projects and wanted to perform them for others outside of their classes. Teachers were apprehensive at first, especially if they had no dance experience. It was a leap of faith to trust the script. Once the teachers saw how the students responded, they were anxious to put their own touches on the lessons and expand the lessons and units. The one prevalent comment is that they wished there were more days in the unit so they could take their time with teaching the skills and allow for more practice. They also thought the students needed more time to work on projects. There is no reason not to break up any of the lessons in this book and use whatever time is available to expand. Suggestions for doing this are included in the extension sections found at the end of most of the lessons.

DANCE AND EDUCATIONAL STANDARDS

Beyond all the benefits of teaching dance, it can be another way of meeting educational standards and expectations. In the United States, the arts are included in the No Child Left Behind Act (NCLB), tacit national recognition that the arts contribute to academic achievement and are a vital part of society. NCLB is a basis for ensuring that dance is provided for and that there is a reason for all students to have dance experiences in their schools.

It is a good idea to become familiar with your local jurisdictional laws and regulations concerning the arts that may provide a basis for having dance instruction in the schools. For example, Maryland has COMAR (Code of Maryland Regulations), which says that all students receive instruction in all four of the arts. Other countries may have their own national and jurisdictional regulations about arts instruction. Every teacher should be familiar with them.

The National Dance Association (part of AAHPERD, the American Alliance for Health, Physical Education, Recreation and Dance) developed as an outgrowth of the Goals 2000: Educate America Act the publication titled *National Dance Standards for Dance Education*. This act made the arts a core subject according to federal law. The standards are goals toward achieving what every young American should know and be able to do in dance. The standards are broken down into grade levels (K through 4, 5 through 8, and 9 through 12). For the purposes of this book, these national dance standards for grades 5 to 8 are listed with each lesson.

The National Dance Education Organization (NDEO) also has the publication *Standards for Learning and Teaching Dance in the Arts: Ages 5-18*. The approach is different from that of the NDA, but NDEO's work is also a good resource for guidelines for dance education.

It should be noted that different standards may be used in different countries and in different jurisdictions or states within a country. A comparison of the Maryland Essential Learner Outcomes in Dance with the National Standards, for example, shows only a few differences. It is certainly possible and wise to incorporate all standards that apply into any dance program.

USING THIS PACKAGE TO TEACH DANCE

This book, DVD, and CD package offers a proven and easy method for bringing the benefits of dance to your middle school students. Three dance units with ready-to-use lessons are presented: improvisation, dance for athletes, and jazz dance. These lessons walk you through the process of planning and teaching a dance unit step by step, from introducing basic dance and fitness terminology to facilitating a student-created group performance at the unit's end.

The lessons are easy for instructors without dance expertise to use. Basic dance terminology and fitness terminology are meshed. Basic dance steps are used that are similar to what students and teachers may already know. Each lesson even features a script that you can follow word for word in class. The script is based on the experience of many teachers using these units and makes even novices feel confident.

Because the lessons have been designed by and for instructors, they address each aspect of the instructional process, from preparation to assessment. Each lesson lists the materials needed, objectives and National Dance Standards met, dance terminology used, and preparation required. Homework and assessment are woven throughout the lessons so that students spend time applying the material and evaluating themselves. Self-assessments, group assessments, and teacher's assessments are included so that both instructors and students can easily gauge students' learning.

The music CD bound into the book takes the work out of selecting music for class work and performances. Songs of various styles and tempos are available to suit the particular needs of your classes. The DVD bound into the book supports the instruction of the lessons with visual aids, student handouts, homework assignments, and rubrics. The DVD also includes video demonstrations of correct technique for the skills taught in the lessons. With the demonstrations, you and your students can know for certain how the skills should be done.

There is continuity from improvisation to dance for athletes to jazz dance. Students will recognize some of these skills and build on them. After teaching the units several times, you will establish your own routine and be able to add your own creativity. You and your students will be amazed and proud of what you create and how your performances improve from grade to grade.

YOU CAN DO IT!

If you are a physical educator, many of the tools you need are already at your disposal:

- Facility: A gymnasium or other large space with appropriate flooring is needed.
- Familiarity with movement skills: Physical educators know basic footwork and coaching cues for a variety of movements and sport skills.
- Knowledge of moving students safely within a space: Physical educators are familiar with drill formations, lines, squads, and the use of equipment.
- Knowledge of anatomy and exercise physiology: Physical educators have been trained to analyze skills and movement from an anatomical and physiological perspective.
- Coaching skills: Physical educators have been trained to coach for improvement.
- Physical fitness, physical education, and dance are a good match because of the fitness components involved in dancing, the similarity of movement, and the discipline necessary for training in dance and sports.

But these units are not just for physical educators—they are easy for anyone to use! You might be someone who

- coaches or has played a sport;
- takes dance, Pilates, yoga, aerobics, or similar classes;
- plays a musical instrument or has a music background;
- enjoys social dance;
- regularly works out at a gym or at home;
- is interested in theater or performance; or
- wants to learn some dance skills with your students.

Teaching dance should be fun for both students and you, the teacher. In this book, DVD, and CD package, the students are given clear instructions, and *they* create dance projects. You are the director, not the dancer. You learn *with* the students.

The dance units in this book have already been taught—and they work. Students have had fun, learned new movement skills that have helped them be better athletes, found an outlet for their creativity, performed their projects, and assessed their work. Your students can have that experience too!

Acknowledgments

This book is based on the middle school physical education dance units taught in Anne Arundel County Public Schools in Maryland. The middle school physical educators were tasked with teaching dance units and asked that the units be "goof proof" for nondancers. After the initial writing, professional development, and actual teaching of the units in tight time constraints, feedback helped in making changes. The groundwork done in AACPS gave me the foundation to write this book.

The school system should be acknowledged for its support of dance. Dance is taught in physical education in kindergarten through fifth grade. Dance units are taught in middle school physical education. Year-long fine arts dance classes are offered to students in grades 6, 7, and 8, and a middle school dance magnet program (by audition) in one area of the county is established with plans for a magnet to service the rest of the county. High schools offer Dance I through IV, Dance for Athletes I through IV, and Dance Company class I through IV (by audition). All high schools have a dance company that performs all year. Many elementary and middle schools also have a dance company that performs in the AACPS dance festivals and at their school. Visit www.aacps.org/dance for information about the dance program.

Carolyn Anderson taught physical education and currently works with the AVID program in Anne Arundel County Public Schools. She became interested in dance and began a dance program, including dance classes and a dance company at the middle school where she taught. She helped write the original version of the units.

Stephanie Atwell taught language arts in Anne Arundel County Public Schools and is trained in dance. She began a dance company at the middle school where she taught and strongly felt that all students should have dance as part of their education. She helped write the original version of the units.

Kathleen Cochran is a physical educator and science educator who taught the initial version of the dance units, saw the positive effect on her students, and helped make adjustments to the original version of the units when the school system changed to 80-minute classes.

Ken B. Dunn, physical education instructor at South River High School, educated me about plyometrics and its value for dancers and athletes. Ken puts plyometrics to practice in all of his classes.

South River Dance Company provided the photo models and the demonstrations for the instructional DVD. Many thanks to director Nicole Deming, the South River Dance Company dancers, and the South River High School administration and HPED department for their help with this project.

Dancers from the South River Dance Company who participated in the making of this book's instructional DVD. Front row, L-R: Kara Halsey, Clare Wood, Samantha Blonder, Ellen McIntyre-Severson, Ashley Krogel, Kelly Olsen. Middle row, L-R: Nicole Canavan, Christine Moren, Lindsay Tarr, Rachel Kramer, Madeleine Raley, Jennifer Snowden, Emily Vitacolonna. Back row, L-R: Marisa Kopack, Cara Ervin, Molly Maloy, Violet Hill, Toivo Tamm, Nicholas Uria, Morgan Mylod, Julia Walker, Sydney Maenner, Alison Quigley, Nicole Deming (director).

Thanks also to Scott Swanson, who took the photographs for this book. His expertise is invaluable.

USING THIS BOOK, DVD, AND MUSIC CD TO TEACH DANCE

You should carefully read this instruction section because it will help you in setting up and managing all aspects of teaching the units on improvisation, dance for athletes, and jazz dance. Everything is included: transforming the facility, transforming students into dancers, using the DVD and CD, understanding how each part of each lesson works, understanding how the lessons within a unit build on each other, using the handouts and signs, managing students' paperwork and projects and performances, assessing students' work, and making adjustments when needed.

SEQUENCE OF UNITS

The units were chosen based on knowledge of students in sixth, seventh, and eighth grades. In some populations, students might relate to any of the units, but the choice here is based on what we know the students would be comfortable doing. Sixth-graders (ages 11 to 12) are still open to trying just about anything and are not yet creatively inhibited by being "cool." Improvisation works with them. Seventh-graders (ages 12 to 13) can identify with sports and might be playing on community or school teams. Dance for athletes builds on familiar territory, including the project students create. Seventh-graders are also increasingly concerned about their appearance, so the fitness aspect (being in shape) is a hook. Eighth-graders (ages 13 to 14) have the "cool" factor going on, and they identify with jazz dance from what they see in the media. (Think *Grease* and *So You Think You Can Dance*.) Jazz dance is also gender neutral, so the complication of having to teach female and male movement is removed.

It is a good idea to teach to the grades for which they were created, at least initially until you see how the students react. If students are open to other units, then the units are suitable for any age. You must teach the lessons in order, because the skills and knowledge build from lesson 1 through lesson 8 (9 in jazz dance).

So let's get started!

TRANSFORMING THE SPACE

First, you'll need to transform the facility into a studio and performance space. Any large space that is clear of obstacles will work: a gym, a multipurpose room, a cafeteria, a stage, and in good climates an outdoor space that is level and smooth. Identifying the walls of the room as if they were a stage (audience, stage right, stage left, downstage, upstage) makes a practice space (studio) and a performance space (stage). The signs are referenced in the lessons where needed and included on the DVD. (If there are mirrors, then that wall should be audience, or downstage.) A student handout, Origin of Stage Directions, explains the layout of a stage and is included with the lessons. Create a word wall featuring the vocabulary used in each unit and a few dance posters and *voilà*, studio. It is important to call the space the *studio* when it is used for learning material and practicing or the *stage* when it is used for performance so that students are immersed in the vocabulary used for the units.

If an outdoor space is used, you can mount the signs on PVC pipe or wooden stakes, and you can put the pipe or stakes in 36-inch (1 m) cones. This will allow you to set the appropriate size of the space (the size of a gym as opposed to the size of a soccer field).

You will need a sound system with enough volume to fill the space. This could be as simple as a boom box or as sophisticated as a Sound Machine (a powerful portable sound system that has a wireless microphone, remote, built-in speakers, variable speed CD or MP3 player, and auxiliary hookups for additional speakers if needed). A remote control is essential so that you can start and stop music without using class time to go back and forth from the sound system to the instruction spot. (Music is discussed later in this section.)

If a budget is available for some enhancements to the space, consider having mirrors installed on one wall with a curtain that can be drawn to cover them. This allows you and the students to see each other while they are learning material, which helps with corrections. It also allows for the mirrors to be covered so that students perform without looking into the mirrors as they would be if performing on a stage. Another enhancement is to have variable-speed capability for sound so that you can slow down the tempo of any music to help students learn the material and speed up the music for a challenge. A third enhancement is to install track lighting above the mirrors. This gives the feeling of stage lighting. None of these items is necessary, but if the budget allows, the feeling of a real studio is nice.

TRANSFORMING THE STUDENTS (AND INSTRUCTOR!)

You need to feel like a dance director, and the students need to feel like dancers. A teacher's attitude makes a world of difference. Your mind-set needs to be such that everyone can move in their own way, dance is movement, and therefore you are all dancers. Your enthusiasm is essential. If you do not have any dance background, you and your students are learning the material together. You need to be willing to do the movement with the students and work on correcting your own technique as you help students correct theirs. "We're all going to have fun learning this together" is the required attitude. You should wear comfortable clothing that allows students to see your movement, but avoid layers of loose, bulky clothes. A warm-up suit with a T-shirt that is tucked in works fine.

Like the teacher, students need to have the right attitude. For some students, *dance* is a dirty word. Students need to understand that they are not taking ballet lessons in these units. They will learn some dance steps, of course, but the steps will be those used in sport and in social forms of dance (for example, line dancing). In some communities, parents of boys are not thrilled that their sons are dancing. You might need to do some public relations initially (explain how athletic ability will improve, for example). Once you teach the units, that will not be an issue. Parents might also be concerned about the sexual nature of jazz dance because of what is seen in the media. The steps and combinations used are gender neutral and rated G (for general audiences).

Students need to be dressed like you: comfortable but such that movement can be seen. Students need to understand that corrections in technique can occur only if you and the students can see the movement. Again, layers of baggy clothing prevent the student and you from seeing and correcting movement. If the units are being taught in physical education class, the school gym suit is fine. Students may ask to wear spandex under their gym shorts for modesty if the shorts have baggy legs. This is a good idea if it makes students more comfortable. If the units are not being taught in physical education, a discussion with students about what clothing is needed and why and specific options are good ideas. Students can work in sneakers or in bare feet if the floor is kept clean. Hair should be out of their faces and secured with barrettes or elastics. Hard and bulky clips and bobby pins that fall out or need constant adjustment are not suitable. A ponytail is suggested for any students with long hair.

Here are items to avoid and reasons for prohibiting them:

- Jeans do not stretch enough and often sit too low on the hips.
- Shirts that are too large can't be tucked in (when a student is inverted the shirt will slide up and bare the midriff). Shirts that are too short won't stay tucked in (when the student raises the arms or stretches, the midriff will be bare).
- Clothing with beading or sequins is unsafe when students work with partners or in groups. The beading and sequins often fall on the floor and make it unsafe for students who are barefoot.
- Belts have buckles or other adornment that could snag or scratch.
- Jewelry falls off, gets lost, and snags on clothing; hoops can be torn out of earlobes.
- Gum causes choking when a student is moving.
- Socks are too slippery on a wood floor.

HANDLING STUDENTS WHO HAVE DANCE TRAINING

There will always be students in your classes who take private dance lessons. Their technique may or may not be correct, but other students will recognize that they can dance. It is important to harness this ability and put it to good use. Students who can count can be leaders, and students who have correct technique for various skills can be models. These students may know more about dance than you, the teacher! Don't be intimidated by this. This is a very good reason to read the script the first time the units are taught. The script is in the language of dance, and students who have dance training will recognize that. Trained students are a good resource for you and can be good coaches for other students.

MANAGING HANDOUTS, SIGNS, AND STUDENTS' WORK

Handouts for students support the instruction and are included on the DVD. When a lesson calls for you to prepare handouts, thumbnail images of those handouts are included for your reference. There are also signs for posting. These allow you to identify certain areas of the space (such as a particular stage direction or workstation) and reinforce important rules and concepts (such as audience etiquette and vocabulary terms). Depending on the method of assessment for the school or school district or system (points, letter grades, percentages), the electronic copy can be copied into a Microsoft Word file so that the suggested point values on assessments can be changed or any other changes can be made. But the first time you teach the units, avoid making changes so that you can determine what alternatives students might need.

Management of the handouts can be tricky. Students will need to refer to their handouts regularly, so taking them home or storing them in their lockers might mean needing extras for every class or having them so wrinkled or torn that they are not usable. This wastes class time. Here are a couple of options.

- **Option 1:** Have the students form their groups for their projects on the first day of the unit as part of your orientation. Have the students choose a name for their group. Make a folder for that group, and keep all of the handouts for the group in that folder. Have paper clips to clip each student's handouts together. Make sure students put their names on their handouts as soon as they receive them so there is no question about which handouts belong to which student. Have a box for the folders for each class. *Advantage:* fewer folders; *disadvantage:* students forget to put their names on handouts and use another student's handout.

- **Option 2:** Have a folder for each student. Put the student's name on each folder, and have a box for the folders for each class. *Advantage:* no mix-ups of handouts; *disadvantage:* lots of folders.

A container holding enough pencils with erasers will be needed in each class. You should keep the container in the same place so students do not waste time getting and putting away pencils. You'll need to keep the pencils sharpened. Pens will not work. As choreography for the projects changes, students will need to erase and make changes to their Pathways Maps, for example.

An easy way to have all of the items handy is to have a rolling cart that holds the boxes of handouts, the container of pencils, and the music player. This is especially helpful if the class is taught in more than one space, and it allows for easy lockup.

The directions in each lesson tell you what you need to duplicate ahead of time and when to hand out each item to students during the lesson.

SEQUENCE AND STRUCTURE OF LESSONS

Each unit builds from the first lesson to the last, so the lessons are to be taught in order. There is a theme to each lesson (such as shapes, fitness components, or isolations). The skills are taught in progression within each lesson, and the skills taught in one lesson carry over to the next lesson. The format of all lessons is the same: outcomes, standards, materials, preparation, vocabulary, the teacher's script and directions (how to manage the class and the body of skills to be taught), closure, and extension. The scripts have been tested for clarity of directions (that is, students understand the directions and can easily follow them). You will present the skills and knowledge in the first several lessons; the later lessons in each unit require students to create a group performance project using what they have learned in previous lessons. Performance and aesthetic criticism are part of each project. Criteria and assessments for all student work are included.

Here are details of each part of the lesson plans:

- **Outcomes.** These are what students should know and be able to do by the end of the lesson. Outcomes are reviewed with students first thing in each lesson. Part of closure is reviewing the outcomes to determine whether they were met and to determine whether students need more time on some material.

- **National Dance Standards.** While these standards (set by the National Dance Association) can be reviewed with students, the actual purpose of listing the standards is advocacy. The existence of national standards in dance validates the teaching of dance. Having the standards listed is valuable when you are being observed teaching or when discussing the classes with administration or other school personnel.

- **Materials and preparation.** Each lesson contains a list of materials needed for that lesson. Some materials are used in multiple lessons and are listed each time so that you do not have to refer to other lessons. The preparation for each lesson is what you need to do ahead of time. If the space is dedicated (that is, if you are using an actual dance studio for your work), you will not need to put up signs daily, which will cut down on preparation time. You will need to allow plenty of preparation time the first time you teach the units.

- **Vocabulary.** The vocabulary listed includes the dance terms that are used in that lesson. They are bolded in the lessons. Students need to learn dance vocabulary and be able to identify dance skills with the correct terms. A student-created word wall is a nice way to decorate the studio. (To make a word wall, assign students a dance vocabulary word; have them research it, or give them information about the word, and then have them create a poster or other art work with the word and its meaning. Manila paper strips for word walls can be found in office supply stores.)

- **Warm-up.** Each lesson clearly identifies how students should be positioned when they enter the class. This is for efficient and safe movement. You will review the outcomes and present the opening script (an overview of what will occur in class that day). This sets the stage for the lesson—students know to tune in to the outcomes and understand what they will do in class.

Each unit has a distinct warm-up routine. This prepares the body for the rest of the class and establishes the class routine. The warm-up in dance for athletes and jazz dance is the same daily. The warm-up in improvisation varies because the students improvise during their warm-up. All warm-up skills are demonstrated on the DVD, and the music for them is on the CD. Use of the DVD and CD is discussed in detail later in this section.

- **Activities.** Each lesson presents a set of skills. For example, students learn about and do a series of locomotor and nonlocomotor movements the first day in improvisation, and they focus on shapes or levels in other lessons. In addition to the warm-up in dance for athletes, students do plyometrics, which help refine and economize movement. In the jazz dance unit, after learning some technique, students learn a jazz dance combination. Each lesson adds more to the combination so students end up with a short dance.

    • **Script.** There are 8 (9 in jazz dance) scripted lesson plans in each unit. As noted previously, each lesson includes a script that you can read word for word when conducting the lesson; these scripts are identified in the lesson by an arrow and vertical rule (see thumbnail for an illustration). When you ask the students questions, possible responses are listed in brackets in the script. The script is supported by clear instructions that guide you in directing students and alert you to situations that might arise.

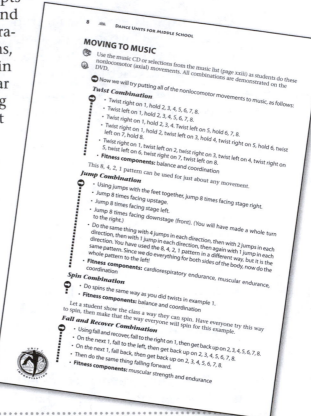

    We recommend that you read over the lessons before teaching the material. The first time you teach the lessons, you should read the script exactly as it is written, especially if you do not have a dance background. The script gives students the correct terminology and cues to help them learn the correct technique. You can place the script on a clipboard for ease of use in class.

    Each lesson is meant to take an hour; however, experience has shown that much more time can be spent on technique and practice. You shouldn't feel as if you are rushing the students. The pace should be what the students need in order to learn the skills with correct tech-

Arrows indicate the teacher's script in each lesson.

nique. Any of the lessons can be broken down into several lessons if time allows and if you would like to spend more time on form. Students regularly want more time to practice skills and rehearse their projects so their performance is more refined.

    • **Closure.** At the end of each class, when making their way to a closure spot, students will do a locomotor movement they have learned. You will review the outcomes and ask questions about the lesson to ascertain students' needs. This refocuses students on what they have learned and what they need to work on. Closure is scripted.

    • **Extension.** Some lessons lend themselves to further activities that enhance achievement, deepen knowledge, challenge students, or perhaps are just fun. Suggestions for extensions are at the end of each script where appropriate. Some classes will progress faster than others, and extensions are a good way to give those classes extra activity to keep all of the classes on the same lesson on the same day. (The word gets around that a class did something neat, and that motivates the slower classes to step it up so they can get to do some extras too!)

TEACHING PLYOMETRICS

The plyometrics in these units is a series of locomotor skills done in a rhythm with good form. These skills improve control of movement, footwork, agility, speed, jumping ability, coordination, and timing—all of which are important for athletes and dancers and for injury prevention. Regular plyometrics as done in these units will help students move more efficiently.

As with the warm-ups, the skills used in plyometrics are demonstrated on the DVD in the sequence taught. When teaching the plyometric skills, you can show the students the demonstration on the DVD, then they can practice to the music on the CD. When you look at the list of skills, it may seem as if there is no need to look at the DVD. But there is! It is the form demonstrated that is important. For example, running isn't just any old run. The form (the way the run is done) and the rhythm improve the students' running ability. Be sure to watch the students carefully and correct form.

Setting up the class for plyometrics and determining the timing for it are explained in detail in the lesson plans. The students must count phrases of 8 beats. You will quickly see which students can easily count beats and which students have difficulty. A suggestion is to have the students who count well in the middle lines and make it their job to count "5, 6, 7, 8" to cue their row to begin on count 1. For clarification, look at the diagram and instructions in the lessons.

FACILITATING STUDENT PROJECTS

Each unit ends with a group project that uses the skills taught. The students create the project based on criteria sheets. In addition to creating the project, students complete a Daily Contribution Sheet indicating what they have contributed to the project that day, a Pathways Map that shows exactly where they travel during the project, a self-assessment, a group assessment, and a critique. You will complete an assessment sheet for each group as well. All of these handouts and forms that you and your students will need are on the DVD.

You will need to make provisions so that each group has a space in which to work, a music source, and time to practice in the performance space. Each group will need access to their folders and pencils while they are working and practicing.

Performance

Each group will have an opportunity to perform their projects for you and the rest of the class. To motivate students to give good performances, you could invite parents to class on performance day, let students invite their other teachers, and invite the principal or other school personnel. This is also good public relations in that it demonstrates what the students have learned and the value of creating and performing. The process through which the performance evolved can also be explained so the invited audience understands what was involved.

It is likely the "stage" will be in the space where the class is held. A stage space should be approximately 36 feet wide by 30 feet deep (about 11 by 9 m). Cones, tape, flags, or other markers can be used to identify the stage space. Performers need to practice in this space several times for safety and to become accustomed to occupying all of the performance space. It is good to have the space marked when students first begin their projects so they have a visual idea of the space that their project should use. The audience needs to sit along the wall with the "downstage" and "audience" signs. If parents or other adults will be in the audience, have some chairs available.

If there is time, you can enhance the lesson by having students review their assessments (self and others), make changes to improve their project, and perform it again. Some groups will be much better rehearsed, have better timing, or have movement that is more interesting. Watching those groups will give students ideas, and being able to rework their project will encourage the weaker groups to improve. The stronger groups will further refine.

Students' absence while the group is working on the project is a problem. If possible, send the project dates home with students at the beginning of the semester with an explanation of what is involved, and ask parents not to schedule appointments on those days. If a student is ill, the rest of the group will have to work around that. Students who miss the project will need to make it up. Possibilities include creating an individual project (if the students are comfortable with that), pairing up with another student who was absent, and working after school, at lunch, or at home. The group might also be willing to get together to work with the absent student and perform their project again.

Audience Etiquette

Audience etiquette is a part of each unit. A sign for the wall that enumerates aspects of proper etiquette is included on the DVD; it can also be given to students as a handout. Before performances, you will review audience etiquette in a lesson. It is also part of the assessment. Students should watch each performance attentively because they have to complete an assessment for it. They should not do anything that would distract a performer (such as making faces or tapping) and should applaud heartily at the end. It is essential for students to understand that everyone is doing their best and that regardless of whether or not the viewer thinks it is good, the performers need to be rewarded for their efforts with applause. This helps build community, encourages everyone to give their best, and teaches respect for others.

Assessing With Criteria Sheets and Rubrics

Students need to know what will be assessed and the value (weight) of each item before they begin their projects. Rubrics that outline the expectations and guide their work on the projects are included on the DVD. You need to circulate while students are working and get a sense of who is contributing and who is not, because points are awarded for contributions and work each day. Students complete a Daily Contribution Sheet each day they work on projects; on the Daily Contribution Sheet, they write exactly what they contributed to the group. You will use these in scoring the contribution section of the assessment.

Self-assessments and group assessments are handouts that are introduced in the lessons at the appropriate time. During a performance, you and the students have an assessment sheet, which is essentially a checklist. While watching the performance, you and the students check off items as you see them. Students also do a self-assessment; in this assessment, what the teacher and others see and what the students think they did should be similar. Students are often more critical of themselves than teachers and classmates are. A final assessment is to write a critique. Guidelines for the critique are on a student handout. If possible, ask the language arts teacher to go over the critique guidelines in language arts class. This could be an interdisciplinary project.

USING THE DVD

The DVD includes demonstrations of all skills lesson by lesson in the order they are taught. Each script includes verbal coaching for technique, and the DVD shows correct technique in the skills. Some students will translate the verbal cues to their bodies, while others will need the visual and the verbal cues. If you have no dance background, you will find the DVD demonstrations invaluable. Once students have correct technique, you can use the music CD instead of the DVD.

The DVD also includes copies of all of the signs, handouts, criteria, assessments, and other forms. You do not need to create any of those materials. Simply print them out from the DVD and you are ready to go. To speed up preparation time, make a clean copy of each item and put them in folders labeled Improvisation, Dance for Athletes, and Jazz Dance so that you can run off items for students. If you can project right from a computer in the studio, students can look at the handout they are working with and see exactly what they are to complete.

It's a good idea to save all handouts and other files to another source right away so that if the DVD is lost or damaged, you still have what you need.

USING THE CD

The accompanying music CD includes music for warm-up, music for plyometrics, selections of music for the projects in each unit, and a selection for the jazz combination. All music is rated G.

The CD has tracks long enough for the warm-ups for any of the units; the tracks come in four speeds: learner, slow, medium, and fast. The slow speed is approximately 130 beats per minute. The medium speed is about 140 beats per minute. The fast speed is approximately 150 beats per minute. It is a good idea to learn the warm-up on the learner speed, which is about 120 beats per minute. Each speed is a different style of music. Once the students have learned the warm-up, vary the speed from day to day among slow, medium, and fast. Varying the speed helps the students learn to control their movement and think about what they are doing rather than warm up on autopilot. It is also a challenge.

There are three speeds suitable for plyometrics: slow, medium, and fast. Both the tracks for warm-up and plyometrics can be used for the skills. The advantage of having music in different speeds on the CD is that you can adjust the tempo to what students need.

The project tracks include a variety of styles of music; all are between 135 and 140 beats per minute. The jazz combination track is at 130 to 135 beats per minute. If students are able to perform the combination faster, the medium or fast tracks for warm-up and plyometrics will work.

To save time, it is a good idea to use the music CD the first time you teach the units. Selecting and editing your own music takes a lot of time, and the tempo is critical.

SELECTING YOUR OWN MUSIC

Teachers face several challenges when trying to find music suitable for dance classes. Following is a discussion of some of the pitfalls in selecting music for class.

The first pitfall is *lyrics*. Much of the current music has lyrics that are not suitable for middle school students. Profanity and references to sexual behavior, drug and alcohol use, violence, and gangs are in the lyrics. Some of the lyrics are in lingo that the students understand but adults do not. It is a good idea to have a trustworthy teenager listen to the lyrics and act as interpreter while you are present. I have had teens tell me not to use music after they listened to the lyrics! Broadway lyrics are often sexually suggestive or refer to subjects unsuitable for middle school students. Rap, hip-hop, and current top 40 need careful screening.

The second pitfall is *tempo*. All of the warm-ups, plyometrics, and combinations require music with even phrases of 8 counts. Many selections of music have uniform phrases but then insert a phrase with a different number of counts. It is hard enough for some students to count sets of 8, much less keep counting when the music is not even. Some selections of music vary the tempo within the song, slowing down and speeding up. Those selections are not suitable for these units.

The third pitfall is your *time*. It takes an inordinate amount of time to listen to music. Once you find a song, you need to screen for lyrics. As just mentioned, it also takes time to find the right tempo. So you have to listen to the entire song before deciding whether it is suitable. Often samples of downloadable music do not include the whole song.

The fourth pitfall is the *length* of the song. Many songs are less than 5 minutes (the warm-up requires a music selection that lasts at least 5 minutes). Songs downloaded or recorded from a CD need to be edited so the phrases of 8 continue from one song to the next if one song is not long enough for the entire warm-up or combination.

Pitfalls discussed, we don't intend to discourage you from selecting your own music; you should just be aware of what is involved in doing it properly. Varying the music maintains students' interest as well as your interest and is a good way to expose students to a variety of music.

Many companies sell CDs for fitness classes and master the music into a steady tempo with sets of 8 counts, usually grouped into 32-count sets. The CDs are available in these genres, among others: '50s, '60s, '70s, '80s, '90s, country, rock, techno, Broadway, Southern rock, drums, top 40, and various artists (such as Beatles). The CDs list the beats per minute, and the songs are blended together so there is no ending or change in tempo, which is great for these units. Some of the music has lyrics that need to be screened, and some of the music is instrumental. Some companies have downloads to MP3s so you can select whatever songs you want at whatever speeds you want. This saves a lot of time! One such company is Dynamix Music (www.dynamixmusic.com).

Another way to save time getting music is to ask students to bring in music they like—with criteria. Tell your students that they need to listen to the whole song and make sure it has the same beat throughout. They also need to print out the lyrics from the Internet (or CD jacket) and bring them in for screening. Note that the lyrics from the Internet are often not the same as those on the CD! Students need to listen to the lyrics as they read them from the printout to make sure they are the same. Students should have read the lyrics before bringing in the music and disqualify anything that refers to the problem items mentioned previously. For example, you can tell students that the class needs selections of music that are over 5 minutes long or that have a fast beat, or you can request a song that makes you want to move. Depending on the community, it might be a good idea to let students know that certain types of music cannot be used for class.

If there is time, students can go on a music hunt and learn about music history. For example, some students might be assigned to talk with their grandparents and bring in a song that their grandparents danced to—with a short report about the music and the dance. Or you can assign a decade or a style of dance and charge the students with bringing in music from that decade (such as from the 1940s) or a song that is used with a certain style of dance (such as the lindy hop). The possibilities are endless.

A word of caution: *Never* play music that a student has brought in unless you listen to it first. The day that you neglect listening to a piece of music will be the day the principal or someone important walks by the class and goes into shock over the lyrics they hear!

SUGGESTED MUSIC

If you wish to choose your own music, consider starting with the following suggested selections, which have been used and are suitable with regard to lyrics and tempo. Not all of the songs are long enough for the warm-up and plyometrics, but they are long enough for the skills work. You can easily use a software program such as SoundForge (there are others) to edit and blend songs of like tempo together to make longer tracks. With a little practice at blending and editing, you can make a variety of CDs of your own.

Compilations

- *Are You Ready to Dance?* 3rd compilation (Epic records).
- *Brilliant! The Global Dance Music Experience*, volume 6 (SBK/EMI).
- *Londonbeat* (Radioactive Records).
- *Pump Up the Jam*, Techtronic (SBK).
- *Total Recall*, Techtronic (SBK/EMI).
- *Workout* (Atlantic).
- *Trance II* (Max Music). (Ask in music shop to hear some trance music. It has a steady beat and few, if any, words.)
- *Jock Jams*. This series has several volumes; any early volumes are pretty safe.

Artists

- Paula Abdul: *Shut Up and Dance*.
- Black Box: *Mixed Up!*
- C+C Music Factory: *Gonna Make You Sweat*.
- Outback: *Dance the Devil Away*.
- Snap: *Welcome to Tomorrow*.
- 'N Sync: Selected tracks; some are slow.
- Backstreet Boys: Selected tracks; some are slow.
- 2 Unlimited: *Get Ready*.
- 2 Unlimited: *Hits Unlimited*.

Note

- Be very aware of words and meanings that refer to drugs, alcohol, tobacco, sex, violence, gangs, and abuse.
- Be aware of songs that might be offensive to a particular culture.
- Ask a middle school student or a high school student you trust to *listen with you first*. They know the current word meanings among the kids, which is often not what adults think it means!
- Ask in your local shop about instrumental CDs with a good steady beat. You might be able to listen before you buy.
- Go online and listen to samples, then download songs. Be sure to listen to lyrics after downloading if the sample does not include the entire song.
- Be aware that one parent complaint about music used in class can adversely affect the program.

ENJOY!

Everything you need for teaching dance units in middle school is at your fingertips. It should be a fun and rewarding experience for you and your students!

DVD CONTENTS
SIGNS AND HANDOUTS

All Units

Audience Etiquette sign
Audience sign
Bring a Pencil sign
Critique Guidelines
Daily Contribution Sheet (Two-Day)
Daily Contribution Sheet (Three-Day)
Daily Contribution Sheet (Multiday)
Downstage sign
Foot and Arm Positions
Origin of Stage Directions
Pathways Map
Pathways Map Instructions
Stage Directions diagram
Stage Left sign

Stage Right sign
Upstage sign
Workstation 1 sign
Workstation 2 sign
Workstation 3 sign
Workstation 4 sign
Workstation 5 sign
Workstation 6 sign
Workstation 7 sign
Workstation 8 sign
Workstation 9 sign
Workstation 10 sign
Workstation 11 sign
Workstation 12 sign

Unit One Improvisation

Improv Cards 1-4
Improv Cards 5-8
Improv Cards 9-10
Improv Cards Basement
Improvisation Project Cards
- The Adventure Project
- Adventure Park Project
- Astronauts Project
- Avalanche Project
- Beach Bum Project
- The Cafeteria Project
- The Championship Project
- County Fair Project
- Diving Project
- The Internet Project
- Love to Shop Project
- Movie Premiere Project
- My Creation Project
- Road Trip Project

- Sound Machines Project
- We're Lost Project
Improvisation Project Rubric (Two-Day)
Improvisation Project Rubric (Three-Day)
Improvisation Project Rubric (Multiday)
Lesson 1 Outcomes
Lesson 1 Vocabulary
Lesson 2 Outcomes
Lesson 2 Vocabulary
Lesson 3 Outcomes
Lesson 3 Vocabulary
Lesson 4 Outcomes
Lesson 4 Vocabulary
Lesson 5 Outcomes
Lesson 5 Vocabulary
Lessons 6-8 Outcomes
Lessons 6-8 Vocabulary
Movement Problem Cards 1-8
Physical Fitness Definitions

Unit Two Dance for Athletes

Choreographing a Dance

Dance for Athletes Warm-Up Chart

Homework Essay

Homework Essay Rubric

Lesson 1 Outcomes

Lesson 1 Vocabulary

Lesson 2 Outcomes

Lesson 2 Vocabulary

Lessons 3-4 Outcomes

Lessons 3-4 Vocabulary

Lessons 5-8 Outcomes

Lessons 5-8 Vocabulary

Physical Fitness Definitions

Plyometrics

Rules for Safe Stretching

Sports Dance Criteria

Sports Dance Group Assessment

Sports Dance Project Rubric

Sports Dance Self-Assessment

Teacher's Assessment of Performance

Unit Three Jazz Dance

Choreographing a Dance

History of Dance

Jazz Dance Choreography Project Groups

Jazz Dance Collage and Homework Essay

Jazz Dance Collage and Homework
   Essay Rubric

Jazz Dance Criteria

Jazz Dance Performance Group
   Assessment

Jazz Dance Performance Self-Assessment

Jazz Dance Project Rubric

Jazz Dance Warm-Up Chart

Lesson 1 Outcomes

Lesson 1 Vocabulary

Lesson 2 Outcomes

Lesson 2 Vocabulary

Lesson 3 Outcomes

Lesson 3 Vocabulary

Lesson 4 Outcomes

Lesson 4 Vocabulary

Lesson 5 Outcomes

Lesson 5 Vocabulary

Lesson 6 Outcomes

Lesson 6 Vocabulary

Lesson 7 Outcome

Lesson 8 Outcome

Lesson 9 Outcomes

Pathways Across the Floor handout

Rules for Safe Stretching

Teacher's Assessment of Jazz Dance
   Performance

DVD Contents
Video

UNIT ONE—IMPROVISATION

Lesson 1—Locomotor Movements

Bouncy Jog

High Skip

Long, Low Run

Gallop

Hop

High, Long Leap

Chassé

Prance

Jump

Lesson 1—Nonlocomotor (Axial) Movements

Twist Combination

Jump Combination

Spin Combination

Fall and Recover Combination

Isolation Combination

Lesson 2

Jog Forward and Backward

Skip Sideways

Run Low and High

Gallop Forward and Backward

Alternate Hopping and Jumping

Alternate Leaping and Running

Prance Forward

Prance Backward

Alternate Skipping and Jumping

Alternate Stepping and Kicking

Lesson 3

Shadowing

Mirroring

UNIT TWO—DANCE FOR ATHLETES

Lesson 1—Warm-Up

Roll Down and Up
Head Circle Right, Head Circle Left
2-Count Jumping Jacks
Reach Overhead
Reach Back
Transition to Floor
Crunches
Oblique Crunches
Leg-Out Crunches
Hug Knees to Chest
Transition to Cobra
Cobra Stretch
Ankle Grab

Transition to Triangle
Triangle Push-Ups
Low Lunge Right and Left
Mountain Climbers
Transition to Butterfly
Butterfly Stretch
Pike Stretch
V-Sit (Straddle)
Transition to Inverted Stretch
Inverted Stretch
Roll Up
Parallel Lunges
Full Warm-Up to Music

Lesson 2—Plyometrics

Form Running Forward
Form Running Backward
Run Forward, Pivot, Run Backward
Run Backward, Pivot, Run Forward
Sideways Slide
Slide With a Pivot
Grapevine
Grapevine With a Pivot

Hop
Jog and Heel Kick
Long Run
Run, Run, Leap, Run
Skip
Jog, Sprint
Sprint, Jog

Lesson 3—Coordination

Isolation Challenge

Lesson 4—Changing Weight

Combination

Lesson 4—Turns

Jump Turn
Three-Step Turn
Paddle Turn

Soutenu
Pirouette

Lesson 4—Other Movements

Triplet
Swing

Fall and Recover

UNIT THREE—JAZZ DANCE

Lesson 1—Warm-Up

Roll Down and Up

Head Circles Right and Left

Head Isolations Right to Left

Head Isolations Up to Down

Head Isolations Left to Right

Head Isolations Down to Up

Head Isolations Tilt Right and Left

Shoulder Isolations Up to Down

Shoulder Isolations Back to Front

Shoulder Isolations Backward Rolls

Shoulder Isolations Forward Rolls

Rib Isolations Right to Left

Rib Isolations Front to Back

Rib Isolations Left to Right

Rib Isolations Back to Front

Rib Isolation Circles Right and Left

Reaches Up Right and Left

Side Reaches Right and Left

Floor Reaches Right and Left

Transition to Floor

Crunches

Oblique Crunches

Leg-Out Crunches

Hug Knees to Chest

Transition to Butterfly

Butterfly Stretch

Transition to Pike Stretch

Pike Stretch

Transition to Straddle Stretch

Straddle Stretch

Transition to Low Lunge

Low Lunge Right and Left

Transition to Parallel Second

Plié and Straighten

Roll Up

Warm-Up to Music

Lesson 2

Jazz Walk

Jazz Run

Jazz Walk and Kick

Grapevine

Combination

Lesson 3

Step–Together–Step–Jump and Clap

Three-Step Turn With a Touch

Stomp and Clap

Paddle Turn

Pas de Bourrée

Combination

Lesson 4

Jazz Square

Slide

Sit Spin

Combination

Lesson 5

Kick–Ball–Change With Lunge

Chassé and Leap

Combination

Music CD Contents

Warm-Ups

These tracks can be used to accompany warm-ups in all three units.

1. Warm-Up Learner (50s style; 120 beats per minute; 6 minutes and 58 seconds)
2. Warm-Up Slow (swing/funky style; 130 beats per minute; 6 minutes and 59 seconds)
3. Warm-Up Medium (country style; 140 beats per minute; 6 minutes and 36 seconds)
4. Warm-Up Fast (techno style; 150 beats per minute; 6 minutes and 55 seconds)

Plyometrics

5. Plyometrics Slow (60s style; 130 beats per minute; 6 minutes and 50 seconds)
6. Plyometrics Medium (R&B/techno/Latin style; 140 beats per minute; 6 minutes and 58 seconds)
7. Plyometrics Fast (70s style; 150 beats per minute; 6 minutes and 48 seconds)

Projects

These tracks can be used to accompany projects in all three units.

8. Project 50s (134 beats per minute; 2 minutes and 53 seconds)
9. Project Broadway (135 beats per minute; 3 minutes)
10. Project Country (135 beats per minute; 2 minutes and 56 seconds)
11. Project Techno (132 beats per minute; 2 minutes and 59 seconds)
12. Project 60s (135 beats per minute; 2 minutes and 53 seconds)
13. Project Disco (135 beats per minute; 3 minutes and 3 seconds)
14. Project Motown (130 beats per minute; 2 minutes and 59 seconds)
15. Project March (128 beats per minute; 2 minutes and 53 seconds)
16. Project Latin (135 beats per minute; 2 minutes and 59 seconds)

Jazz Combination

17. Jazz Combination (funk; 132 beats per minute; 2 minutes and 51 seconds)

Note: Warm-up and plyometrics tracks can be interchanged. The jazz combination can be done to any track with a similar BPM.

UNIT ONE

IMPROVISATION

1

INTRODUCTION, LOCOMOTOR WARM-UP, AND NONLOCOMOTOR SKILLS

OUTCOMES

- Students will become familiar with stage directions.
- Students will be able to identify locomotor and nonlocomotor movements.
- Students will be able to identify fitness components that improve as a result of the activities.
- Students will be able to perform a variety of locomotor and nonlocomotor movements to music.

NATIONAL DANCE STANDARDS

- Identifying and demonstrating movement elements and skills in performing dance
- Making connections between dance and healthful living
- Making connections between dance and other disciplines

MATERIALS

- Music with a steady beat and appropriate words (see music CD or suggested selections on page xxiii)
- Music player with enough volume for class space

- Physical Fitness Definitions

- Stage Directions Diagram handout

- Origin of Stage Directions handout

- Audience, Stage Right, Stage Left, Upstage, and Downstage signs
- Audience Etiquette sign
- Laptop and projector if projecting handouts

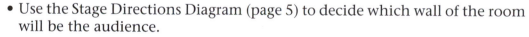

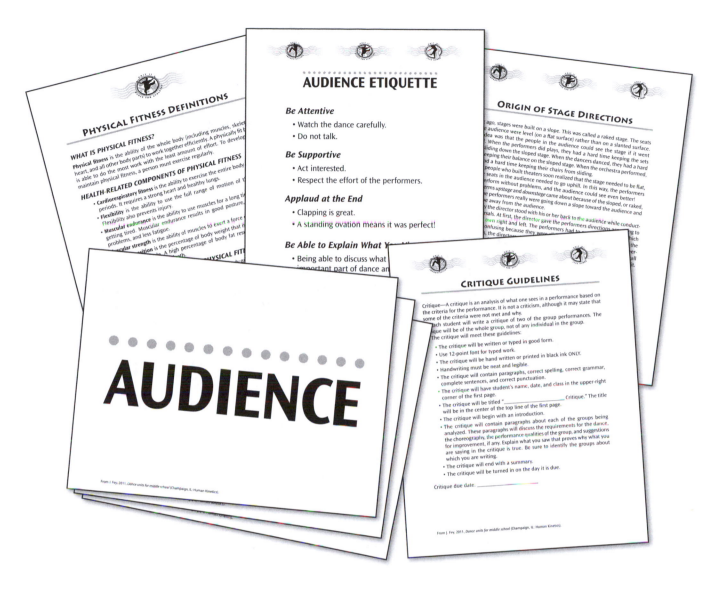

PHYSICAL FITNESS DEFINITIONS

WHAT IS PHYSICAL FITNESS?

Physical fitness is the ability of the whole body (including muscles, skeleton, heart, and all other body parts) to work together efficiently. A physically fit body is able to do the most work with the least amount of effort. To develop and maintain physical fitness, a person must exercise regularly.

HEALTH-RELATED COMPONENTS OF PHYSICAL FITNESS
• **Cardiorespiratory fitness** is the ability to exercise the entire body for long periods. It requires a strong heart and healthy lungs.
• **Flexibility** is the ability to use the full range of motion of the body. Flexibility also prevents injury.
• **Muscular endurance** is the ability to use muscles for a long time without getting tired. Muscular endurance results in good posture, fewer back problems, and less fatigue.
• **Muscular strength** is the ability of muscles to exert a force.
Body composition is the percentage of body weight that is fat compared to lean muscle. A high percentage of body fat results in poor health.

...ICAL FITN...

AUDIENCE ETIQUETTE

Be Attentive
• Watch the dance carefully.
• Do not talk.

Be Supportive
• Act interested.
• Respect the effort of the performers.

Applaud at the End
• Clapping is great.
• A standing ovation means it was perfect!

Be Able to Explain What Y... ...
• Being able to discuss what ...
...important part of dance an...

ORIGIN OF STAGE DIRECTIONS

...ago, stages were built on a slope. This was called a raked stage. The seats ...e audience were level (on a flat surface) rather than on a slanted surface. ...dea was that the people in the audience could see the stage if it went ... When the performers did plays, they could see the stage if it went ...liding down the sloped stage. When the dancers danced, they had a hard time keeping the sets ...keeping their balance on the sloped stage. When the orchestra performed, ...d a hard time keeping their chairs from sliding. ...people who built theaters soon realized that the stage needed to be flat, ... seats in the audience needed to go uphill. In this way, the performers ...erform without problems, and the audience could see even better! ...rms *upstage* and *downstage* came about because of the sloped, or raked, ...e performers really were going down a slope toward the audience and ...e away from the audience. ...y the director stood with his or her back to the audience while conduct-...rsals. At first, the director gave the performers directions a...g to ...own right and left. The performers had to...which ...onfusing because they were...the ...s, the director...er-...all...

CRITIQUE GUIDELINES

Critique—A critique is an analysis of what one sees in a performance based on the criteria for the performance. It is not a criticism, although it may state that some of the criteria were not met and why.
...ach student will write a critique of two of the group performances. The ...que will be of the whole group, not of any individual in the group.
...The critique will meet these guidelines:
• The critique will be written or typed in good form.
• Use 12-point font for typed work.
• The critique will be hand written or printed in black ink ONLY.
• Handwriting must be neat and legible.
• The critique will contain paragraphs, correct spelling, correct grammar, complete sentences, and correct punctuation.
• The critique will have student's name, date, and class in the upper-right corner of the first page.
• The critique will be titled "_____ Critique." The title will be in the center of the top line of the first page.
• The critique will begin with an introduction.
• The critique will contain paragraphs about each of the groups being analyzed. These paragraphs will discuss the requirements for the dance, the choreography, the performance qualities of the group, and suggestions for improvement, if any. Explain what you saw that proves why what you are saying in the critique is true. Be sure to identify the groups about which you are writing.
• The critique will end with a summary.
• The critique will be turned in on the day it is due.

Critique due date: _____

From J. Fey, 2011, *Dance units for middle school* (Champaign, IL: Human Kinetics).

AUDIENCE

From J. Fey, 2011, *Dance units for middle school* (Champaign, IL: Human Kinetics).

PREPARATION

• Run off enough handouts for all students.

• Use the Stage Directions Diagram (page 5) to decide which wall of the room will be the audience.

• Post stage direction signs and Audience Etiquette sign.

• Post outcomes for the lesson.

• Post the vocabulary for the lesson.

• Give the Critique Guidelines sheet to the language arts teachers, and ask them to go over it with students as part of language arts class. Do this before or at the beginning of the unit (or at the beginning of the school year) so there is plenty of time to incorporate this into the language arts class.

UNIT 1
IMPROVISATION

VOCABULARY

- downstage
- upstage
- stage right
- stage left
- center stage
- improvisation
- 5, 6, 7, 8
- walk

- jog
- skip
- run
- gallop
- hop
- leap
- chassé
- prance

- jump
- locomotor
- nonlocomotor (axial)
- twist
- spin
- fall
- recover
- isolation

LESSON INTRODUCTION

Seat students in lines facing stage right. If you use squads, it will be easy to turn the squads around to face the wall that is stage right. The students should be sitting on the left side of the room (stage left) facing the right wall of the room, as follows (example shows a class of 30 divided into 5 lines of 6 students each, facing stage right):

Audience

X X X X X X

X X X X X X

X X X X X X

X X X X X X

X X X X X X

Make the distance between lines as large as the space permits.
After students are seated, review the outcomes for the lesson.

➡ We are starting a dance unit on **improvisation**. This means that you will make up your own movements. There is no right or wrong—you can have fun with just about any safe movement you want!

The movement in this unit will improve your physical fitness just like all of the other activities in physical education class, athletics, or any other type of fitness class. It will also help you if you are in sports, drama, music, or dance because it will improve your ability to play and perform.

Pay close attention to the kinds of music used during this unit. You will use music for your improvisation project. Be able to identify the kind of music you would like to use for your project later in our unit.

These are the stage directions, which you will need to know: **downstage, upstage, stage right, stage left,** and **center stage**.

To help you remember the stage directions, I will tell you a story about why the stage directions are labeled as they are.

Read students the story in the Origin of Stage Directions handout.

➡   We will use stage directions for our dance unit.

Point to walls and ask students to call out stage right, stage left, and so on, until they become automatic.

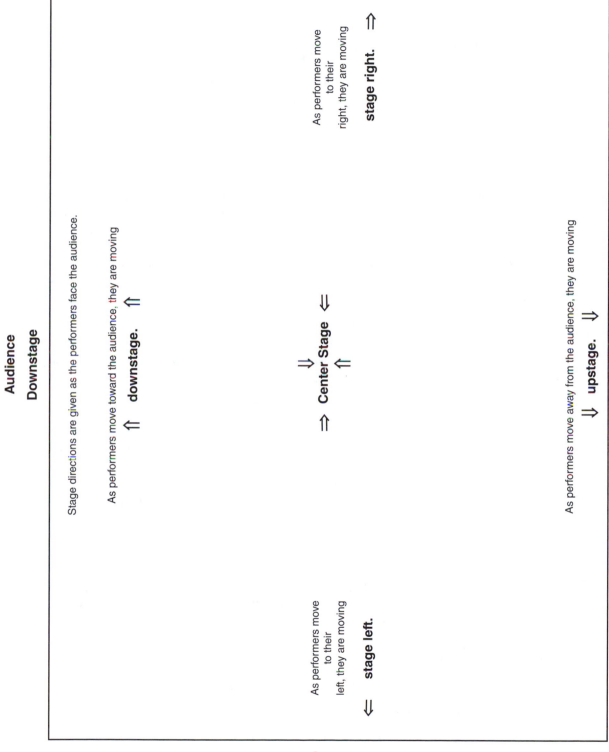

Stage Directions Diagram.

WARM-UP

➡ Now we will warm up by traveling across the floor with music. Movements that travel are called **locomotor** movements.

This is the method for traveling across the floor with music. The music will be in phrases of 8 counts. Each movement begins on count 1. I will start the movement by calling out, "**5, 6, 7, 8,**" so you can feel the beat. From stage left, you will start each movement on your right foot on the count of 1. From stage right, you will start on your left foot on the count of 1. The first row will begin and do the movement all the way across the floor. The second row will count and begin 8 counts after the first row. The third row will count and begin 8 counts after the second row. Each group always begins their movement on the count of 1, and all steps are on the beat of the music. This pattern will continue until all groups have moved across the floor. As each row finishes the movement, they will line up to come back across the floor. Everyone is to stay in his or her line at all times and count at all times. Are there any questions about how we move across the floor?

Review and ask questions to make sure students understand. Put on music, call out, "5, 6, 7, 8," and have each row clap on count 1 when it is their row's time to begin the movement.

➡ We will begin with walking on the beat. Everyone is to count sets of 8 aloud softly while they are waiting their turn and while they **walk**. First we will start with the right foot and walk *over,* which means from stage left to stage right. When all have finished and are lined up on the stage right side, I will call out, "5, 6, 7, 8," and the first group begins walking back, starting with the left foot. *Back* means from stage right to stage left.

Students do this. It might take some practice to have everyone begin on count 1. Stopping the music and starting again may be necessary. Some students will do the movement at the speed their bodies want to do it rather than on the beat. This is the time to establish each row coming in on count 1 without pauses between sets of 8 counts, starting with the correct foot, and keeping the movement on the beat before the movement is more complicated than walking.

➡ Now that you have the idea and are coming in on time, we will try different movements over *and* back. Remember to start with the right foot from stage left and the left foot from stage right, come in on count 1, and stay on the beat. I will call out each movement before we do it and cue you with "5, 6, 7, 8." Think about the fitness components that each movement could improve. We will talk about them at the end of class.

 Try the following movements. All are demonstrated on the DVD.

➡ • **Jog.** The movement should be bouncy.
  • **Skip.** Try to go as high as you can.
  • **Run.** Use long, low strides.
  • **Gallop.** This is a step–together long movement, resembling the way a horse runs.

- **Hop.** Jump on one foot all the way across, or change feet halfway across.
- **Leap.** Run 3 steps and then leap. The leap should go high and long; leaps will alternate legs.
- **Chassé.** This is step–together–step. In a chassé one foot literally chases the other foot. The steps are long, short, long; the count is "1 and 2." To begin, step forward with your right foot on 1, the left foot steps next to the right foot (chasing it) on "and," then the right foot recovers on 2 by taking another long step. The left foot begins the next chassé on 3, the right foot chases the left on "and," then the left foot takes another long step on 4. (Count 1 and 2, 3 and 4, 5 and 6, 7 and 8.) [Note: Chassé can be done either with the feet staying on the floor or leaving the floor on "and." Students with dance training may automatically go in the air. If this happens, either let students choose, or decide that everyone does it one way or the other.]
- **Prance.** This is a bouncy movement resembling a horse trot.
- **Jump.** Jump with both feet together all the way across the stage.

As the lessons go by, you will get really good at these movements because you have been _____ [practicing]. Today was easy. I will be calling out combined movements in the lessons ahead, so you have to pay close attention.

Now that you are warmed up, spread your lines across the space—as far apart as the room permits. The leaders walk forward and everyone else follows to spread out.

What you did across the floor are locomotor, or traveling, movements. Now you will do some movements in place. These are called **nonlocomotor,** or **axial,** movements—movements that do not travel and that move around the axis of the body. Try these, doing 8 of each together as a class, without music. I will start you with "5, 6, 7, 8." Be sure to start on count 1 and stop after 8.

Try each of the following. (Before students try the fall, be sure to explain the concept by reading the description to them.)

- **Twist.** Right and left, upper body, standing in place.
- **Jump in place.** You can have the feet together, apart, or one in front of the other.
- **Spin in place.** Spin right, spin left, on two feet, on one foot.
- **Fall.** A fall is a change in body position from standing, kneeling, or sitting to a position on the floor. A fall generally is a sudden movement but can be done gradually. When you fall, your weight should rest on the thigh, buttock, side of the leg, or back of the shoulder rather than on the knee, elbow, or base of the spine. You can fall in different directions, from different levels, and with changes in speed, energy, and weight. [Be sure to show students the demonstration of the fall and recover combination on the DVD so they know how to execute the movements safely.] Try a slow fall to one side, **recover** (get up), then fall to the other side, then try a slow fall back, then try a slow fall forward.
- **Isolations.** Move *only* one part of your body at a time. Try moving only the head R, L, R, L, R, L, R, L (8 counts).

MOVING TO MUSIC

  Use the music CD or selections from the music list (page xxiii) as students do these nonlocomotor (axial) movements. All combinations are demonstrated on the DVD.

 Now we will try putting all of the nonlocomotor movements to music, as follows:

Twist Combination

- Twist right on 1, hold 2, 3, 4, 5, 6, 7, 8.
- Twist left on 1, hold 2, 3, 4, 5, 6, 7, 8.
- Twist right on 1, hold 2, 3, 4. Twist left on 5, hold 6, 7, 8.
- Twist right on 1, hold 2, twist left on 3, hold 4, twist right on 5, hold 6, twist left on 7, hold 8.
- Twist right on 1, twist left on 2, twist right on 3, twist left on 4, twist right on 5, twist left on 6, twist right on 7, twist left on 8.
- **Fitness components:** balance and coordination

This 8, 4, 2, 1 pattern can be used for just about any movement.

Jump Combination

- Using jumps with the feet together, jump 8 times facing stage right.
- Jump 8 times facing upstage.
- Jump 8 times facing stage left.
- Jump 8 times facing downstage (front). (You will have made a whole turn to the right.)
- Do the same thing with 4 jumps in each direction, then with 2 jumps in each direction, then with 1 jump in each direction, then again with 1 jump in each direction. You have used the 8, 4, 2, 1 pattern in a different way, but it is the same pattern. Since we do everything for both sides of the body, now do the whole pattern to the left!
- **Fitness components:** cardiorespiratory endurance, muscular endurance, coordination

Spin Combination

- Do spins the same way as you did twists in example 1.
- **Fitness components:** balance and coordination

Let a student show the class a way they can spin. Have everyone try this way to spin, then make that the way everyone will spin for this example.

Fall and Recover Combination

- Using fall and recover, fall to the right on 1, then get back up on 2, 3, 4, 5, 6, 7, 8.
- On the next 1, fall to the left, then get back up on 2, 3, 4, 5, 6, 7, 8.
- On the next 1, fall back, then get back up on 2, 3, 4, 5, 6, 7, 8.
- Then do the same thing falling forward.
- **Fitness components:** muscular strength and endurance

Note: Fall and recover is very tiring. You might want to have the students wait for 8 counts in between each fall and recover if you have a class that seems hesitant or is in less than optimal physical condition. Have the students take a deep breath in between the falls if you wait 8 counts. Twice through the exercise is plenty for any group.

Isolation Combination

- Using the pattern right, left, down, up, move the head on the counts of 1, 3, 5, 7. Do this twice.
- Now use the pattern left, right, up, down and move the head on the counts of 1, 3, 5, 7. Do this twice.
- Now try to put the right and left together, doing the right twice and the left twice without any stopping in between.
- After you master that, try it on every count.
- Use the same timing for the shoulders, ribs, and hips, but use these patterns.
  - Shoulders: up, down, front, back; then down, up, back, front.
  - Ribs: front, back, right, left; then back, front, left, right.
  - Hips: right, back, left, front; then left, back, right, front.
- Now let's hook the patterns all together with no break. This will take some practice. These are called isolations. [Watch to make sure students only move the designated body part.]
- **Fitness component**: coordination

CLOSURE

Do a locomotor movement to come over and sit down in your lines, like you did at the beginning of class.

- In each of the examples we just completed, name the fitness components we improved.
- Name the stage direction as I point to it. [Point to downstage, stage right, stage left, upstage, and center stage.]
- Name four locomotor movements.
- Name four nonlocomotor movements.
- We will be doing a group project, starting with lesson 5. Be sure to listen to the music in each lesson so you know which music your group would like to use for the project.
- Did we meet our objectives for today? Why not, if no?
- What was hard and what was easy? What could you do to improve? [Students should mention practice.]
- I encourage you to practice everything at home that we did in class so you can do it better the next time we have class.

> Here is the Origin of Stage Directions handout and the Stage Directions Diagram handout. These review what we learned at the beginning of class and will help you with your project. Here is the Physical Fitness Definitions handout too. What are the skill-related components of physical fitness? [Students read from handout.] What are the health-related components of physical fitness? [Students read from handout.] We will be identifying physical fitness components as we learn dance skills. Please take one of each and put it in your folder on your way out. Good class!

Note: Do not worry if you do not cover all of this in the first lesson. Depending on the students and the length of the class, you may be able to cover only part of it. Choose from each section what you think the students will enjoy most if time is limited. Extend the lesson into another class period to cover everything thoroughly if time is not limited.

EXTENSION

Assign or let students select a vocabulary word from the lesson. Students will artistically create a word for the word wall.

2

WARM-UP, GRAPH PAPER, AND CHANGING SPACES

OUTCOMES

- Students will identify fitness components that improve as a result of the activities.
- Students will increase proficiency in the unit warm-up movements.
- Students will be able to perform a variety of movements to music.
- Students will experience the relationship between space and movement.
- Students will create their own movements.

NATIONAL DANCE STANDARDS

- Identifying and demonstrating movement elements and skills in performing dance
- Applying and demonstrating critical-thinking and creative-thinking skills in dance
- Making connections between dance and healthful living

MATERIALS

- Music with a steady beat and appropriate words (accompanying CD or see suggestions on page xxiii)
- Music player with enough volume for class space
- Four distinctly different pieces of music for Changing Spaces
- Tape, cones, numbers, or flags for Changing Spaces

PREPARATION

- Review Stage Directions Diagram.

- Post stage direction signs and Audience Etiquette sign (if not previously posted).

- Have Stage Directions Diagram and Origin of Stage Directions handouts ready for students absent from lesson 1.

- Post outcomes for the lesson.
- Post vocabulary for the lesson.

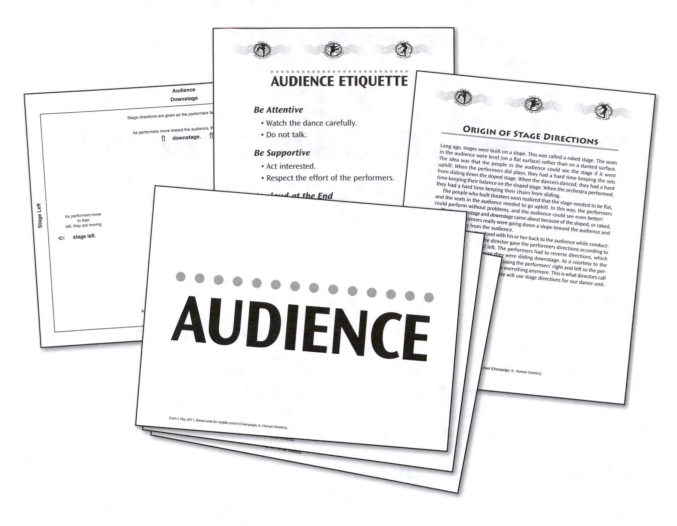

Origin of Stage Directions

Long ago, stages were built on a slope. This was called a raked stage. The seats in the audience were level (on a flat surface) rather than on a slanted surface. The idea was that the people in the audience could see the stage if it went uphill. When the performers did plays, they had a hard time keeping the sets from sliding down the sloped stage. When the dancers danced, they had a hard time keeping their balance on the sloped stage. When the orchestra performed, they had a hard time keeping their chairs from sliding.

The people who built theaters soon realized that the stage needed to be flat, and the seats in the audience needed to go uphill. In this way, the performers could perform without problems, and the audience could see even better!

The terms *upstage* and *downstage* came about because of the sloped, or raked, stage. The performers really were going down a slope toward the audience and up a slope away from the audience.

The director stood with his or her back to the audience while conducting. This meant the director gave the performers directions according to the director's right and left. The performers had to reverse directions, which was confusing because they were sliding downstage. As a courtesy to the performers, directors began using the performers' right and left so the performers didn't have to reverse everything anymore. This is what directors call stage directions. We will use stage directions for our dance unit.

From J. Fey, 2011, Dance units for middle school (Champaign, IL: Human Kinetics).

AUDIENCE ETIQUETTE

Be Attentive
• Watch the dance carefully.
• Do not talk.

Be Supportive
• Act interested.
• Respect the effort of the performers.

Stage Left

Audience

Downstage

Stage directions are given as the performers fa...

As performers move toward the audience, th...
⇑ **downstage.** ⇑

As performers move to their left, they are moving
⇐ **stage left.**

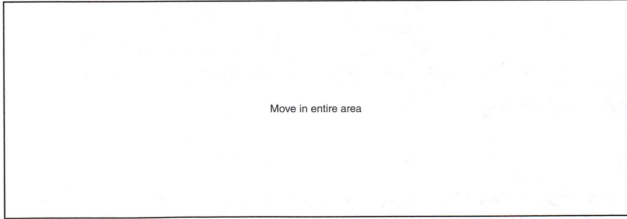

From J. Fey, 2011, Dance units for middle school (Champaign, IL: Human Kinetics).

For the Changing Spaces Activity

Section off the floor. This can be accomplished with tape previously placed on the floor, with cones, with numbers, or with flags. Not all facilities are the same, so section off your movement space in a manner that best suits your needs.

• First mark the entire movement space as follows:

Move in entire area

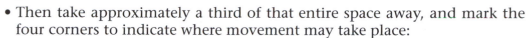

- The four corners should be marked to indicate where movement may take place.
- Then take approximately a third of that entire space away, and mark the four corners to indicate where movement may take place:

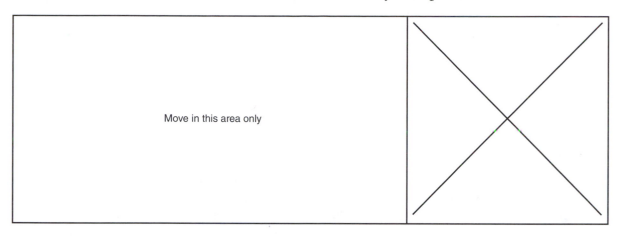

Move in this area only

- Look at the entire space, take approximately two-thirds of that space away, and mark the four corners to indicate where movement may take place.

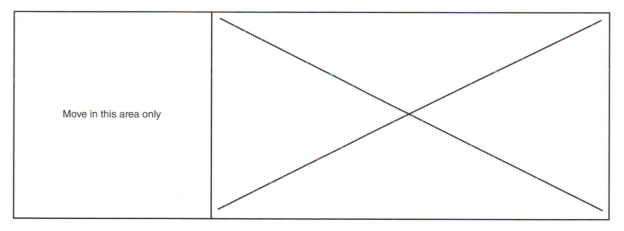

Move in this area only

- At this point you are left with one-third of the entire room.
- Next, take away half of the remaining one-third of the room and mark the four corners to indicate where movement may take place.

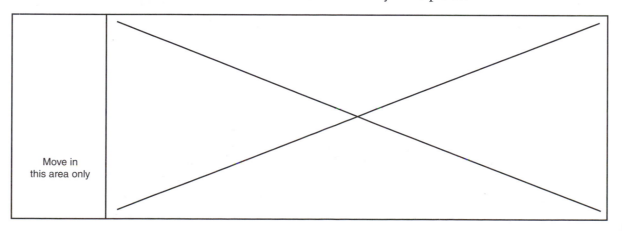

Move in this area only

- Section off a small area out of the remaining space. Again, be sure to mark the four corners to indicate where movement may take place.
- For every section of movement space you create, you will need one piece of music. For example, the previously described setup would need a total of four pieces of music. The change in music will indicate to the students the next change in movement space.

VOCABULARY

- space
- levels
- pathways
- step kick

LESSON INTRODUCTION

When students enter the room, seat them in lines facing stage right. If you use squads, it will be easy to turn the lines around to face the wall that is stage right. The students should be sitting on the left side of the room (stage left) facing the stage-right wall of the room, as follows (example shows a class of 30 divided into 5 lines of 6 students each, facing stage right):

Audience

X X X X X

X X X X X

X X X X X

X X X X X

X X X X X

Make the distance between lines as large as the space permits.
Review the outcomes for the lesson.

➲ This is lesson 2 of our improvisation unit. Can you tell me the stage directions we learned yesterday? [Point to downstage, upstage, stage right, stage left, and center stage and ask students to identify.] Who can tell me why upstage and downstage are named that way? Which foot begins from stage left when we go across the floor? Which foot begins from stage right when we go across the floor?

The movement today will improve your physical fitness just like all of the other activities in physical education class, athletics, or any other type of fitness class. It will also help you if you are in sports, drama, music, or dance because it will improve your ability to play and perform.

Pay close attention to the music used in class so you can make a good choice for your group project.

WARM-UP

➲ We will warm up going across the floor. Yesterday we did simple movements. Today we'll start combining the movements. Remember that I will start the movement with "5, 6, 7, 8" to start the first row, then each row comes in 8 counts after the row in front of them. Make sure you come in on the count of 1 on the correct foot, count the entire time, stay on the beat, and do the movement all the way across the room. These are the movements for today:

Lead students through these movements across the floor. All of the following movements are demonstrated on the DVD.

- Jog forward halfway across, then turn and jog backward the rest of the way across.
- Skip sideways over and back, facing the audience the whole time to use both sides of the body.
- Do 4 low runs, then 4 high runs, then 4 low runs, then 4 high runs all the way across the room.
- Gallop (step–together) forward halfway across, then turn and gallop backward the rest of the way.
- Alternate hopping and jumping all the way across (hop R, jump on both, hop R, jump on both over, then hop L, jump on both, hop L, jump on both back).
- Alternate leaping and running all the way across the room.
- Prance 4 forward, then prance 4 in a circle R; prance 4 forward, then prance 4 in a circle R until across the room. Circle to the left on the way back.
- Prance backward all the way across.
- Alternate skipping and jumping all the way across (skip 4, jump 4, skip 4, jump 4).
- Alternate stepping and kicking all the way across (step R, kick L, step L, kick R). You can choose what kind of kick (karate, high, low, sideways, backward).

Now that we are warmed up, do any locomotor movement to come over to your lines and sit down. Today we'll do two activities using space. **Space** is the area in our room. Sometimes we have a lot of space to move in, and other times we have only a little space. Sometimes we are spaced evenly, like in our lines. Sometimes the space can be at different **levels**. Right now sitting in your lines, you are in low-level space. If you were standing, what level would you be in? [High.] Movement can occur at all levels, and we'll work on levels in another lesson.

GRAPH PAPER

Imagine that our floor has lines on it like a piece of graph paper. The rules are that everyone has to move only along the lines of the graph paper. You can imagine the lines as close together or as far apart as you want, but you must move only along the lines of your graph paper. This would mean that everyone would only be moving in what kind of line? [Straight.] The line on which you move is called a **pathway**. Another rule is that there can be no collisions and no talking. This means that everyone has to keep the eyes open and use the eyes to signal which person will turn away if two people are heading directly for each other. What kind of turn would it need to be? [Sharp, 90-degree turn, or 180-degree turn.] The last rule is that we have to fill up all of the space in the room, so everyone has to watch and move toward empty space all of the time. Okay, let's review the rules. What are they?

- Move only in straight lines along graph paper. That means when you turn, it is a sharp turn!
- No talking.
- No collisions.
- Fill up all of the space in the room.

We will try this with walking to the beat of the music first. When we can do this, then we will add some other movements and rules!

Turn on music, count "5, 6, 7, 8," and students start walking on count 1. Keep reminding students about the rules. They will have a hard time at first. Stop the music a couple of times and regroup. You will see curved pathways and turns and empty space until students have practiced for a while. Keep the walk going for a couple minutes, then ask students to walk as fast as they can and still follow the rules. Practice this for a minute or two.

➡ Using the same rules, let's try to do graph paper with jogging. Now let's try it with running.

Students do it about a minute while you cue them to fill up all space and jog only on the lines of the graph paper.

Note that students who are not in shape may get out of breath. This is a good time to point out and explain the fitness component. [Cardiorespiratory endurance: getting out of breath makes the heart muscle stronger so it can pump more blood with each beat and not work as hard.]

➡ Everyone have a seat right where you are. How did we do on moving only along straight lines? [Students respond.] How about avoiding collisions without talking? [Students respond.] How about filling up all of the space? [Students respond.]

We will try it with jogging and a different rule now. The music will stop now and then. When the music stops, find a way to go down to the floor (fall, lower level), making sure not to collide with someone else. When the music starts, get up (recover, higher level) and continue jogging along your graph paper.

Students do it, and you stop music four or five times.

➡ You did very well (or we need to work on) filling up space. You also did well (or we need to work on) moving in straight pathways and avoiding collisions. Some other time we might try the same thing using curved pathways only. Now we'll do another activity about space.

CHANGING SPACES

➡ What would happen if suddenly you had less space? [Possible responses from students are "I'd have to put away or give away some of my things to make room" and "I'd feel crowded."]

What would happen if suddenly you had more space? [Possible responses from students are "I'd feel freer," "It would be easier to move," and "It would be easier to organize things."]

Today we are going to look at movement space and how that affects movement. As you can already see, there are cones (or tape, numbers, or flags) around the movement space.

Preview the movement spaces with students and explain how the areas are sectioned off.

Using the movements we've already done in class, or using any other safe movement you would like to use, I want you to move all around the space and take up all of the space until you hear the music change. When you hear the music change, the movement space will get smaller, and you must then move within the next cones (tape, numbers, flags). Every time the music changes, your movement space gets smaller. As you move, I want you to think about what you are doing and how you feel each time the space gets smaller.

Proceed with the activity and stop when students are in the smallest space. To ensure that students are moving in the correct space, stand in the non-movement area (preferably closest to the movement area) to monitor.

Now that you are all in a very small space, we will reverse the activity and have the space grow. When the music changes, the space grows. As soon as the space grows, be sure to take up all of the space right away. Again, pay attention to your movement and how you feel as the space gets larger.

Proceed with activity.

CLOSURE

Do any locomotor movement you want over to your lines and have a seat.

- How did you feel when you could move using the entire space? [Freer, could do larger or faster movement, easier not to bump into others.]
- How did you feel when space was taken away from you? [Had to move carefully, smaller, felt constrained or uncomfortable.]
- Did you notice any changes in your movements? When? Explain.
- How should you move in a crowded classroom or hallway?
- How did you feel when the space got larger again? Why?
- Do you prefer crowded space or open space? Why?
- Did we meet our outcomes for today? If not, why not?

EXTENSION

If more time exists, allow students to do this experiment with changing spaces *before closure*. Place your arms at a 90-degree angle. Start with students in the smallest space and have them look at how your arms frame the space and determine its size. Move away a little and have students look at how their space increased as determined by your arms. Explain that the space is no longer measured by the cones (or tape, numbers, flags) and is going to get bigger and smaller and also change locations based on your arms. Their assignment is to do any safe movement and fill up all of the space as it changes. Stay at one size of space for 10 to 15 seconds until the students get used to their new space. Do this a couple times, then begin to move the space continually (smaller, larger, side to side). It is a real challenge to change the movement to fill up all the space as it constantly changes.

3

WARM-UP, LEVELS, SHADOWS, AND MIRRORS

OUTCOMES

- Students will identify fitness components that improve as a result of the activities.
- Students will increase proficiency in the unit warm-up movements.
- Students will be able to perform a variety of movements to music.
- Students will experience the relationship between levels and movement.
- Students will create their own movements.

NATIONAL DANCE STANDARDS

- Identifying and demonstrating movement elements and skills in performing dance
- Applying and demonstrating critical-thinking and creative-thinking skills in dance
- Making connections between dance and healthful living
- Making connections between dance and other disciplines

MATERIALS

- Music with a steady beat and appropriate words (accompanying CD or see suggestions on page xxiii)
- Music player with enough volume for class space

- Cards labeled 1 to 10 and Basement
- Optional: Deal-a-Dance cards (These cards are included with the book *Building Dances: A Guide to Putting Movements Together* by Susan McGreevy-Nichols, Helene Scheff, and Marty Sprague. The cards work well with this lesson, but they are not necessary for conducting the lesson.)

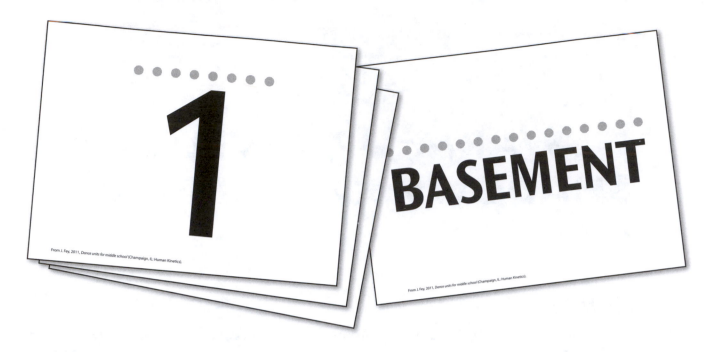

From J. Fey, 2011, *Dance units for middle school* (Champaign, IL: Human Kinetics).

From J. Fey, 2011, *Dance units for middle school* (Champaign, IL: Human Kinetics).

PREPARATION

- Post list of music used.

- Laminate cards 1 to 10 and Basement.
- Optional: Laminate Deal-a-Dance cards.

- Post outcomes for the lesson.
- Post vocabulary for the lesson.
- Devise a way to partner students for the Shadows and Mirrors activity.

VOCABULARY

- shadowing
- mirroring

LESSON INTRODUCTION

When students enter the room, seat them in lines facing stage right. The students should be sitting on the left side of the room (stage left) facing the right wall of the room, as follows (example shows a class of 30 divided into 5 lines of 6 students each, facing stage right):

Audience

X X X X X X

X X X X X X

X X X X X X

X X X X X X

X X X X X X

Make the distance between lines as large as the space permits.
Go over the outcomes for the lesson.

➡ This is lesson 3 of our improvisation unit. Can you tell me the stage directions we learned? [Point to downstage, upstage, stage right, stage left, and center stage.] Who can tell me why upstage and downstage are named that way?

The movement today will improve your physical fitness just like all of the other activities in physical education class, athletics, or any other type of fitness class. It will also help you if you are in sports, drama, music, or dance because it will improve your ability to play and perform.

Pay close attention to the music used in class so you can make a good choice for your group project. The list is posted.

We will warm up going across the floor, combining the movements. Remember that I will start the movement with "5, 6, 7, 8" to start the first row, then each row comes in 8 counts after the row in front of them. Make sure you come in on count 1, count the entire time, stay on the beat, and do the movement all the way across the room.

Lead students through these movements:

➡
- Jog forward halfway across, then turn and jog backward the rest of the way across.
- Skip sideways over and back, facing the audience the whole time to use both sides of the body.
- Do 4 low runs, then 4 high runs, then 4 low runs, then 4 high runs all the way across the room.
- Gallop forward halfway across, then turn and gallop backward the rest of the way.
- Alternate hopping and jumping all the way across (hop R, jump on both, hop R, jump on both over, then hop L, jump on both, hop L, jump on both back).
- Leap R, run L, leap R, run L all the way across, then leap L, run R, leap L, run R back.
- Prance 4 forward, then 4 in a circle, then 4 forward, then 4 in a circle until across, then reverse back.
- Prance backward all the way across and back.
- Skip 4, jump 4, skip 4, jump 4 all the way across and back.
- Step R, step L, kick R all the way across. You can choose what kind of kick (karate, high, low, sideways, backward). Step L, step R, kick L all the way back.

LEVELS

➡ Go to your line (squad) spots for this activity. [Students go.] Think about things that you see that have different levels to them. [Students respond: parking garages, malls, stadiums, schools.] Today we will explore moving at different levels.

How many of you have ever been in an elevator? Today we'll use the concept of elevators to explore levels of movement.

Think of your bodies as elevators. Lie on the floor. [Students do this.] This is your basement level. Now, stand up on your toes with your arms stretched to the ceiling. [Students do this.] This is your 10th floor. Lower your elevator now to the 5th floor. [Students do this.] Where is your 5th floor? Why? [Students respond.]

Now you will determine levels for the rest of the floors in your elevator. I will turn on the music and call out a floor. Move so your body is on that floor. [Turn on music and call out, "Basement." Hold 8 to 16 counts in the music, then call out, "1st floor." Hold 8 to 16 counts in the music, and follow this pattern for 2nd floor, 3rd floor, and so on, to the 10th floor. Stop music.]

I will randomly hold up numbered cards for the floor levels and basement (cards 1 to 10 and Basement). Watch closely. When I hold up a card, quickly reach that floor. [Hold up cards; students move to that floor.]

Now that we know where all of our floors are, we are ready for the elevator to suddenly drop down several floors as if it were falling. Our body elevators will be falling, but let's discuss again what falling is and how to fall without injury. We did this in our first lesson. A fall is a change in body position from standing, kneeling, or sitting to a position on the floor. A fall generally is a sudden movement but can be done gradually. When falling, the weight should rest on the thigh, buttock, side of the leg, or back of the shoulder rather than on the knee, elbow, or base of the spine. You can fall in different directions, from different levels, and with changes in speed, energy, and weight.

Okay, everyone to the basement. [Students do it.]

Slowly show cards, increasing floor numbers until getting to 10. Next show floor 7. Let students fall to floor 7 and then bring students slowly back up to floor 10 again (8, 9, 10). Then show floor 4, and then bring students slowly back up to floor 10 again (5, 6, 7, 8, 9, 10). Next show floor 2, and bring students slowly back up to floor 10 again. Finally, call out floor 1, and have students fall to the basement.

➡ Let's try some other types of falls and levels.

Pick from the following list, or refer to Deal-a-Dance cards if you have them. Call out the items and have students respond by improvising the movement suggested:

- Trying to get something out from under a bed
- Trying to get something from inside a bottom cupboard
- Picking the stars out of the sky
- Catching the moon
- Climbing a tree
- A boat with a hole in the bottom of it
- Caught in quicksand
- Stepping in mud

- A rock that has been dropped in water
- A waterfall
- Tripping up the stairs
- A leaf falling off a tree

➡ Good job. Have a seat. Now we'll do another activity called Shadows and Mirrors.

SHADOWS AND MIRRORS

 Both shadowing and mirroring are demonstrated on the DVD.

➡ Can anyone guess what **shadowing** is? [Movement where one person moves just like the shadow of another.] Let's try shadowing as a group. I would like a volunteer to help with this. [Have the student stand with his back to the class, and make sure everyone is facing the audience.] John (name of student), please move your right hand anywhere, and everyone in the class take your right hand and make it move exactly like the shadow of John's right hand would move. John, now move your head any way you like, and everyone shadow that movement. Does everyone understand? [Answer any questions.]

Some others will have turns as the leader as we work on shadowing. If you are the leader, move slowly at first so we can make our shadows accurate. We will stand in our lines (squads) to do this, so everyone do a locomotor movement to their lines. [Students move to lines (squads).]

Who would like to lead first? The leader stands in front of the group and begins to move slowly standing in place, using any nonlocomotor movement. Move arms, legs, head, or trunk. Try twisting, bending over, reaching up, or leaning. The rest of the class should try very hard to make *exact* copies of our leader's movements. [Let the leader go on for a while, then let a couple other students be the leader.]

Now we will make it harder. This time, our leader may use locomotor (traveling) movements, but travel slowly and not very far at first. Wherever our leader goes, we have to try to do the exact movement as if we were the shadow. [Let the leader move awhile, emphasizing slowly. Students will have a hard time following turns and changes of direction. Stop and try movements again if necessary to get the correct shadow. Some students may figure it out; use them as models.]

Good job. Everyone have a seat. What was the easiest movement to shadow? What was the hardest movement to shadow? Why? How do you think people become good at shadowing movement? [Practice.] Why would being good at shadowing help an athlete? [Defense.] How would it help a dancer or someone in a marching band? [Unison.]

Now we are going to try **mirroring**. What is the difference between shadowing and mirroring? [Shadow = same; mirror = opposite.] I would like a volunteer to help me demonstrate mirroring. We are going to stand facing each other. John (student's name), do a few easy movements with your hands and arms. Notice that as John does these movements, I am moving the way John's image in a mirror would be moving. John, move your head, and I'm going to mirror that. Notice that anytime the person turns, the mirror mover has to turn the opposite way, just like the image in the mirror would. Thank you, John.

We are going to work in partners for this activity. All of the partners will face the same way John and I just did. The partner stage left will be the leader for a couple of minutes. The leader needs to move slowly at first until you get the idea of reversing the movements. [Students mirror for a short time.] Now the partner stage right will lead, and again move slowly at first. [Students mirror for a short time.] Now we will change back to the original leader and try locomotor movements, remembering to go very slowly. [Students do this for a short time.] Now we will change leaders again and try locomotor movements. [Students do this for a short time.] Now, I challenge you and your partner to travel across the room using turns and levels *and* mirroring. When you arrive at your destination, both partners sit down. [Roam around the room and help those having a hard time reversing movement. If you notice a pair doing very well, stop the class and have them demonstrate. If you notice everyone having trouble turning, stop the class, and have two students demonstrate being coached by others in the class.]

CLOSURE

➔ Do a locomotor movement to come over and have a seat. Let's review today's lesson.

- What are levels?
- Did you learn to shadow and mirror?
- Which was more difficult? Why?
- Are you improving your warm-up movements?
- What will help you become a better mover? [Practice.]
- Tomorrow we will work on creating movement from words and stories.
- Did we meet today's outcomes?
- What was hard and what was easy about our class today?

EXTENSION

If time permits, allow students to improvise a dance in partners or in small groups using levels, shadowing, and mirroring. Play music while they work. If students are comfortable sharing their dance, have them take turns performing while the rest of the class watches and identifies levels, shadowing, and mirroring.

4

WORD WARM-UP AND MAKING A MOVIE

OUTCOMES

- Students will identify fitness components that improve as a result of the activities.
- Students will increase movement proficiency.
- Students will be able to create movements from word meanings.
- Students will be able to create a series of movements from a story.

NATIONAL DANCE STANDARDS

- Identifying and demonstrating movement elements and skills in performing dance
- Understanding dance as a way to create and communicate meaning
- Applying and demonstrating critical-thinking and creative-thinking skills in dance
- Making connections between dance and healthful living
- Making connections between dance and other disciplines

MATERIALS

- 1 piece of notebook paper for each group of 5 students
- 1 pencil for each group of students (groups of 5)
- A long list of adjectives and adverbs
- Optional: Deal-a-Dance cards from the green section, numbers 155 to 161 and 181 to 186 (if available)
- Workstation signs

PREPARATION

- Post outcomes for the lesson.
- Post vocabulary for the lesson.
- Devise a way to divide students into groups of 5 (minimum of 4 students, if numbers do not work out in even groups of 5).

- Post Workstation signs so groups are separated when students are ready to write.
- Post stage directions and Audience Etiquette signs (if not already posted).
- Create a list of adjectives and adverbs.
- Optional: Laminate Deal-a-Dance cards (if available).

VOCABULARY

- performance
- audience etiquette

LESSON INTRODUCTION

When students enter the room, seat them in their lines (squads) facing the audience.

Review the outcomes for the lesson.

WORD WARM-UP

➡ Today our warm-up will use all of the space in the room, movements we have used before, and words to give us ideas for different ways to move. It works like this: There is no music. There is no right or wrong movement; anything safe is fine. I will call out a movement, such as *walk*. Everyone will do that movement keeping all of the space in the room filled like we have done before. Then, I will call out a word. Your job is to change or improvise your movement to make it represent the

word. For example, if we were walking, and the word was *droopy,* then you might walk in a way that would mean droopy to you. Everyone could have a different way of representing the word, and that is what we want. Some of the movements people might do could be funny, but we will concentrate on what we are doing, not talking, and filling up all of the space. Stand up in your place and let's try it. Remember, no collisions!

Filling up all of the space, begin walking. [Every 20 to 30 seconds, call out another word from your list of adjectives and adverbs (or any of the Deal-a-Dance cards). Remind students about talking, getting silly, filling up space, concentrating on their own movement, and interpreting the word.] Now prance and let these words help you create movement. [Call out more words.] Now spin. [Call out more words.] Now zigzag. [Call out more words.] Now skip. [Call out more words.] Now run. [Call out more words.]

Note: The options are endless. Use any movements you want, and any words you want. This gets pretty wild, and the students will tire out quickly if they are not in shape. Let them know it is all right to be out of breath.

➡ Which fitness components did you work on with your warm-up? [Students respond. Individuals may have addressed different components.]

Do a locomotor movement back to your lines (squads) and sit down. It's time to make a movie.

MAKING A MOVIE

Determine groups, assign designated workstations, and give each group a piece of paper and writing implement.

➡ I know that all of you have watched a movie at some point in your life. What kinds of movies might you see at the movie theater? [Wait for students' responses: drama, comedy, action, romance, documentary.] Movies also tell stories.

Today you will create a movie with your group. I need to give you a few guidelines before you get started.

- When you write and perform your movie, it must be safe and appropriate for school. [Emphasize this point and ask students to give examples of what might not be appropriate for school. For example, the movement should not depict shooting or stabbing someone.]
- Each group member must play an active part in the movie.
- There will be *no talking, only movement,* during your movie.

You will have approximately 5 minutes to write the story for your movie. Right now I want you to quickly and quietly go to your workstation and sit in a small circle. You may move now. [You might have already placed paper and a writing utensil in work areas, or you may select one member from each group to obtain necessary supplies for his or her group.]

Now you are in a circle with your group, at your workstations. Your group is ready to create the story for your movie. Here is how to do that. Do not begin until we go over all of the directions! The person in the group whose last name

is closest to the end of the alphabet will write the first sentence of your story, and then pass the paper and pencil to the person seated to the left. The second person will then read silently what the first person wrote and write the second sentence to continue the story. When the second person is finished, pass the paper and pencil to the person seated to the left. The third person will read the first and second sentences of the story silently and create a third sentence. This process will be repeated until all group members have contributed. Each group will complete five sentences. If you have four people in your group, then the first person to write will also write the fifth sentence. If you are in a group of five, then each person will write one sentence.

Before you actually write your stories, let's make sure that you understand how to pass the paper and pencil. The person in the group whose last name is closest to the end of the alphabet will write his or her name and sentence on the paper and then pass the paper to the person to the left. That person will then write his or her name and sentence on the paper and pass it to the person seated to the left. Repeat this process until everyone has written his or her name and there are five sentences on the paper. Be sure to write your name next to your sentence. Each person will have 1 minute to complete a sentence. Begin to write the story for your movie. [Students do this. Monitor talking.]

Any questions or problems? Now you will have 5 minutes to write down the *movement* for your stories. Keep in mind that each person must be moving during your whole movie. The movie should be appropriate for school, and it must be safe. You will *not* have people speaking during your movie, only bodies moving. Any questions? Begin. [Keep track of time and monitor groups.]

You have written down what is going to happen during your movie, but now you need to create a way for your bodies to tell your movie story. You will have 10 minutes [maybe 15 minutes—determine by monitoring student progress] with your group members to tell your story through safe movement. Your movie should be no longer than 2 minutes. Begin! Be sure to practice your movement as a group several times so you can perform your movie. [Allow students time to create their movements.]

 Do a locomotor movement to come over and have a seat in the audience area. Bring your papers and pencils to me. [Collect these.] Each group will now perform their movie. Let's quickly review the Audience Etiquette sign to remind ourselves of good **audience etiquette** before groups perform. [Review audience's expectations with class. Randomly select groups to perform.]

After each **performance**, insist that the audience clap. Then ask the audience to do the following:

- Interpret what they saw happening.
- Create an appropriate title for the movie.

Note: This lesson may extend into the following class.

CLOSURE

- Was it easy or difficult to make movement from words?
- How did the words help?
- How did having words make it difficult?
- What fitness components did we work on today?
- Tomorrow we will work on timing and problem solving in movements.
- Did we meet today's outcomes?

EXTENSION

If the movies turn out well and students are enthused about performing them, have students add to their movies and practice them. Consider adding music and costumes. Invite parents, other teachers, or faculty members to come to class for the performance. Ask the invitees to interpret what they saw and to create a title for the movie.

5

COUNT WARM-UP, MOVEMENT PROBLEMS, GROUP TANGLE

OUTCOMES

- Students will identify fitness components that improve as a result of the activities.
- Students will experience stopping and starting movements rhythmically.
- Students will be able to perform a variety of movements to music.
- Students will be able to solve written movement problems.

NATIONAL DANCE STANDARDS

- Identifying and demonstrating movement elements and skills in performing dance
- Applying and demonstrating critical-thinking and creative-thinking skills in dance
- Making connections between dance and healthful living
- Making connections between dance and other disciplines

MATERIALS

- Music with a steady beat and appropriate words (accompanying CD or see suggestions on page xxiii)
- Music player with enough volume for class space

- Movement Problem cards
- Workstation signs
- Basketball or other ball (to be placed at station 1)

PREPARATION

- Laminate Movement Problem cards 1 to 8.
- Post 8 Workstation signs around the space.

MOVEMENT PROBLEM

CARD 1

group must travel across the class space while
a ball the whole time they are moving. While
only 2 people may walk. Only 4 hands may touch
but everyone must have another form of contact
ball in order to travel.

- Post Movement Problem cards in the 8 workstations. Cover the Movement Problem cards so students cannot see them.
- Devise a way to divide students into even groups of 5 or 6.
- Assign each group to a starting workstation.

- Post outcomes for the lesson.

- Post vocabulary for the lesson.

VOCABULARY

- timing
- negative space
- tableau (if extension is done)

LESSON INTRODUCTION

When students enter the room, seat them in lines (squads) facing the audience. Review outcomes for the lesson.

COUNT WARM-UP

In today's warm-up we will work on improving coordination and **timing** by doing a variety of movements on certain counts only. We will work with sets of 8 counts. Sometimes, we will move only on count 1, or only on count 7, or maybe on counts 5 and 6. I will call out which counts have movement. We have to count the music carefully and concentrate to make our bodies move on exactly the count we want. As usual, fill up all of the space and avoid collisions. Make sure all your steps are large and travel far.

Let's start out walking. Take one step on every beat. [Students walk for a minute and count 1 to 8 over and over. Stop music.] Now we are only going to take a step on count 2. Ready? [Start music. Count, calling out 2 loudly. Have students count loudly too.] Now let's try walking only on 3, 5, and 7. [Students try it.] Can you move only on counts 1 and 7? [Students try it.] How about a real challenge? Try counts 3, 4, and 6. [Students try it. Stop music.] Now we'll try the same thing with running. Start out by running on every beat, and then listen for the numbers. [Use any numbers you want. Give students a minute to adjust to and perfect the new numbers before changing numbers again. Review the fitness components of cardiorespiratory endurance and coordination.]

Note: Try these other movements to challenge classes who get the idea quickly: prance, skip, jump, hop, gallop, chassé, and any movement they choose. The warm-up should last until students are sweaty. Some will tire quickly.

MOVEMENT PROBLEMS

Do a locomotor movement to come over and have a seat. Now we will work on solving movement problems. You will work with groups to find solutions to movement problems. Your solutions can be found in teamwork and movement. You will have 4 minutes to go to your station, read your problem, and work out a solution with your group members. One of the problems has a new vocabulary term: **negative space**. [To demonstrate negative space, have a student stand up and put her hands on her hips. Have another student put his hand in the empty space between one of the arms and the torso. The empty space is negative space. Have a few other pairs of students demonstrate until you are sure students understand the concept. Then have five students get up and make a shape using negative space—no one should be touching. To make sure they have the concept, ask students if the whole class could make a shape using negative space.]

When you get to your first station, uncover the movement problem that is posted on the wall. After the groups have solved the movement problem at their assigned stations, we will try another movement problem. [Send groups to the stations you wish and give the signal to begin solving the movement problem. Rotate groups to stations to try as many problems as time permits. Monitor progress throughout. If you see a group doing a very creative solution, stop and have them demonstrate for the class.]

Problems

These are the problems posted and covered at the stations.

Problem 1

The entire group must travel across the class space while touching a ball the whole time they are moving. While traveling, only 2 people may walk. Only 4 hands may touch the ball, but everyone must have another form of contact with the ball in order to travel.

Problem 2

The entire group must travel across the class space while creating and changing the group shape 5 times. The entire group must start in one shape and change to

a new shape while moving. Two people in the group may disconnect in order to change into a new shape, but the rest of the group must stay connected as they move to the new shape.

Problem 3

The entire group must rotate clockwise while traveling across the class space. Every 2 to 5 seconds (teacher decides based on size of space) you may walk using your feet, but the rest of the traveling must use another locomotor movement. You must travel along a straight pathway.

Problem 4

The entire group must travel across the class space entirely connected. While connected, 4 feet may touch the floor, 1 person may not use their legs at all, 1 person may not use their arms at all, and the group has to completely turn 2 times.

Problem 5

The entire group must change levels constantly as it travels across the class space. While changing levels, the group must have 3 hands connected, 3 feet connected, and 3 heads connected.

Problem 6

With only 2 feet touching the floor, move the entirely connected group across the class space.

Problem 7

Move the group across the class space using locomotor movements that change timing 5 times and have at least 3 members of the group connected at all times with body parts other than their hands.

Problem 8

The entire group must move across the class space changing shapes and filling negative space. Group members may not connect at any time.

 Come over and sit in the audience area. [Students do this.] Now we will try a whole-class problem called Group Tangle.

GROUP TANGLE

- Make a line with the whole class and join hands. These hands may not come apart during the whole problem, so hold tightly.

- The students on both ends of the line are the leaders. Their job is to weave in, out, over, under, and through other students (negative space) *very slowly* to completely tangle up the group. You will have to crawl through legs, carefully step over arms, turn, and so on to follow the leaders and tangle.

- When the group is hopelessly tangled up so tightly that no one can move, the whole group works as a team to unravel the group. You must talk quietly to each other about the idea you have to try to untangle yourselves, and all hands must be held the whole time. The problem is solved when the class is back to the original line.

Hint: Place two students at the ends that you know will really try to tangle and won't be shy about going through tiny spaces to do the tangle. Help them find ways to tangle. Insist on slow movement so no one is put in an unsafe position.

Hint: If you have a very large class, you may want to divide the group into 2 smaller groups, or try a boys' tangle and a girls' tangle.

Hint: This is the most fun with 25 to 30 people.

CLOSURE

➡ Do a locomotor movement to come over and sit down.

- What did you learn about movement today? [Timing, negative space.]
- What did you learn about solving movement problems? [Work as a group.]
- What fitness components were involved in the group tangle? [Flexibility, coordination.]
- What fitness components were involved in the warm-up? [Cardiorespiratory endurance, coordination.]
- Tomorrow we will start our group projects.
- Did we meet today's outcomes?

EXTENSION

If time permits, explore negative space by having the whole class make a tableau using negative (empty) space. A **tableau** is a pose—in this case a large one. Demonstrate negative space again by putting one hand on your hip. Then stick your other hand into the space between your arm and torso. Your hand is in negative space. Ask students to give or show some other examples of negative space. Start with one student making any shape he wishes. Let another student volunteer to go next and add to the tableau using only negative space. Encourage creativity and finding space that may not be readily apparent (such as between another student's arms or legs). Remind students that they will not be touching anyone even though they might be intertwined. As each student adds to the tableau, they need to hold still so the next student can find the space he wants to fill. Keep going one student at a time until the whole class has made their tableau. Take a picture of the tableau and post it in the class. The students will be interested in seeing the tableaus from the other classes!

6, 7, & 8

IMPROVISATION PROJECT

The student project for this unit can be completed in three lessons (6, 7, and 8), although more lessons can be added if you think it necessary. Lists of outcomes, National Dance Standards, and materials immediately following this paragraph apply to all of the project's lessons; each lesson has its own distinct preparation.

OUTCOMES

- Students will create their own movement.
- Students will work cooperatively in small groups.
- Students will complete Pathways Maps and Daily Contribution Sheets.
- Students will perform for an audience.
- Students will demonstrate being a conscientious audience member.
- Students will write a critique of their own work and the work of others.

NATIONAL DANCE STANDARDS

- Identifying and demonstrating movement elements and skills in performing dance
- Understanding choreographic principles, processes, and structures
- Understanding dance as a way to create and communicate meaning
- Applying and demonstrating critical-thinking and creative-thinking skills in dance
- Making connections between dance and healthful living
- Making connections between dance and other disciplines

MATERIALS

- CDs used during lessons 1, 2, 3, 4, and 5
- Music player with enough volume for class space

- Improvisation Project cards
- Pathways Map handouts
- Pathways Map Instructions handout
- Daily Contribution Sheet (Three versions are provided for you to choose from, depending on how many lessons you will allow for the project: two days, three days, or more.)

PATHWAYS MAP INSTRUCTIONS

Name_____

Class_____

ADVENTURE PARK
IMPROVISATION PROJECT CARD

Your staff has been given as much money as you need to create the most
theme park in the world. After years of work, you and your staff
people are ready for the grand opening of your theme park.

• The grand opening must take 2 to 3 minutes.
• Each staffer must write a Daily Contribution Sheet (an out
her contributions to the group).

CRITIQUE GUIDELINES

Critique—A critique is an analysis of what one sees in a performance base
the criteria for the performance. It is not a criticism, although it may state
some of the criteria were not met and why.

Each student will write a critique of two of the group performance
will be of the whole group, not of any individual in the group.
critique will meet these guidelines:

e critique will be written or typed in good form.
e 12-point font for typed work.
e critique will be hand written or printed in black ink ONLY.
ndwriting must be neat and legible.
e critique will contain paragraphs, correct spelling, correct g
plete sentences, and correct punctuation.
critique will h

AUDIENCE ETIQUETTE

Be Attentive

• Watch the dance care

IMPROVISATION PROJECT
(TWO-DAY)

Student name_____

Item	Possible point
Day 1 work, effort, creativity	15
Day 2 work, effort, creativity	15
Daily Contribution Sheet	10
Pathways Map	10
Required elements	20
Performance qualities shown	20
shown	10

PATHWAYS MAP

Name_____

Class_____

DAILY CONTRIBUTION SHEET
(TWO-DAY)

Name_____

Class_____

Day 1 contributions
_____
_____
_____
_____
_____
_____

WORKSTATION
1

From J. Fey, 2011, *Dance units for middle school* (Champaign, IL: Human Kinetics).

BRING
A PENCIL
TO CLASS

From J. Fey, 2011, *Dance units for middle school* (Champaign, IL: Human Kinetics).

 • Rubrics (As with the Daily Contribution Sheets, three versions are provided, depending on how many lessons you will allow for the project: two days, three days, or more.)

 • Critique Guidelines
• Paper clips
• Pencils
• Folders numbered for each project group (or each student)
• Audience Etiquette sign
• Bring a Pencil sign
• Workstation signs

PREPARATION

- If not already done, give the Critique Guidelines handout to the language arts teachers, and ask them to go over it with students as part of language arts class. It is best to do this before or at the beginning of the unit (or at the beginning of the school year) so there is plenty of time to incorporate this into the language arts class.
- Place CDs chosen by students in the performance area.

- Laminate Improvisation Project cards.
- Write due date on the Critique Guidelines handout before copying.
- Copy enough Pathways Map handouts, Pathways Map Instructions handouts, Daily Contribution Sheets, Critique Guidelines handouts, and Improvisation Project Rubrics for all students. Note: Copy Pathways Map and Pathways Map Instructions on opposite sides of one sheet of paper.

- Post workstation signs (number of stations are dependent on number of groups).
- Label folders for each project group (or each student) in each class.
- Post Audience Etiquette sign.
- Post Bring a Pencil sign.
- Post outcomes for the lesson.
- Post vocabulary for the lesson.
- Determine the method of grouping students for the project (three to five students per group). Use the project cards or any other method that works for your classes.

VOCABULARY

- unison
- canon
- Pathways Map
- Daily Contribution Sheet
- rubric

=========== **LESSON 6** ===========

LESSON INTRODUCTION

When students enter the room, seat them in lines (squads) facing the audience. Go over the outcomes for the lesson.

➡ For the last three (or more if time permits) lessons of our improvisation unit, we will work on a project in small groups. We will spend a few minutes going over the project requirements before we begin to work on the project. Each group will create a movement combination from an Improvisation Project card. [Hold up pack of cards.] The cards have the requirements for the movement and the project on them. I will read you the titles of the projects to give you an idea of the project choices. Each group will have a different project, so no two groups will use the same project card. [Read titles from cards.]

You have been asked to listen carefully to the music used in class, because today you are going to tell me which music you would like to use for your project. Once you are in your groups, decide very quickly as a group which music you would like, and one person from the group will come up and tell me the music choice.

Also as part of the project, each person will complete a Pathways Map and a Daily Contribution Sheet. I will hand out these sheets and we will go over them. Do not write anything on the sheets until I give the directions. [Pass out Pathways Maps, Pathways Map Instructions, Daily Contribution Sheets, and pencils for those who did not bring pencils to class.]

Neatly write your name and class period on the Pathways Map and Daily Contribution Sheet. [Students do this.] Let's look at the **Daily Contribution Sheet** first. Each day, as you work on your projects, write what you, personally, have contributed to the group on your Daily Contribution Sheet. Completing the Daily Contribution Sheet completely and accurately is a part of the assessment for the project, so you want to do a good job.

Now turn the **Pathways Map** over. This side is an example of how someone might do his or her Pathways Map. It is *not* for anyone to copy. The box represents the performance space. Locate the audience. Look in the lower-right corner of the paper and find the word *start*. When you start working in your group, you will write *start* in the place on the floor where you, personally, start to move. The arrows show the pathway and direction you move. You will see that the student in the example drew an arrow from 1 *start* to 3, and wrote along the arrow line in box 2 what movement she did along that pathway. Look at 3. In the example, the student wrote the movement that she did in this location. From 3, she took a crazy pathway to 5. And along the arrow line, in box 4, she wrote the movement she did while traveling along this pathway. Does everyone understand how to complete a Pathways Map? [Answer any questions.] Keep your Pathways Map with you, and as your group plans their movement for the project, write your own pathways on your Pathways Map. It may be that as your group creates your project, your own Pathways Map will change. Be sure to use pencil so you can erase and make changes.

At the end of each class, everyone will turn in a Pathways Map and a Daily Contribution Sheet. If there are no questions, move to sit with your project group.

Students get into groups. You may assign groups ahead of time, assign projects ahead of time, or use some other method to determine groups and projects. Use what you know will be the most efficient with your students.

I will lay out the project cards and you may select a project for your group. The Improvisation Project cards are very specific about the projects. You may do the project your own way; there is no right or wrong movement as long as you meet the project criteria. You are encouraged to be very creative with your movement. Your movement should not pantomime (which means act out). Work as a group to decide how your group will meet the criteria on the project card. By the end of class today, you should have made decisions about how to do the project. Make sure the movement you make up for your project is appropriate and safe.

Before we begin, we need to go over one of the criteria on the project sheets: The project may not be done in unison. **Unison** means everyone doing the same

PATHWAYS MAP INSTRUCTIONS

Name_____ Class_____

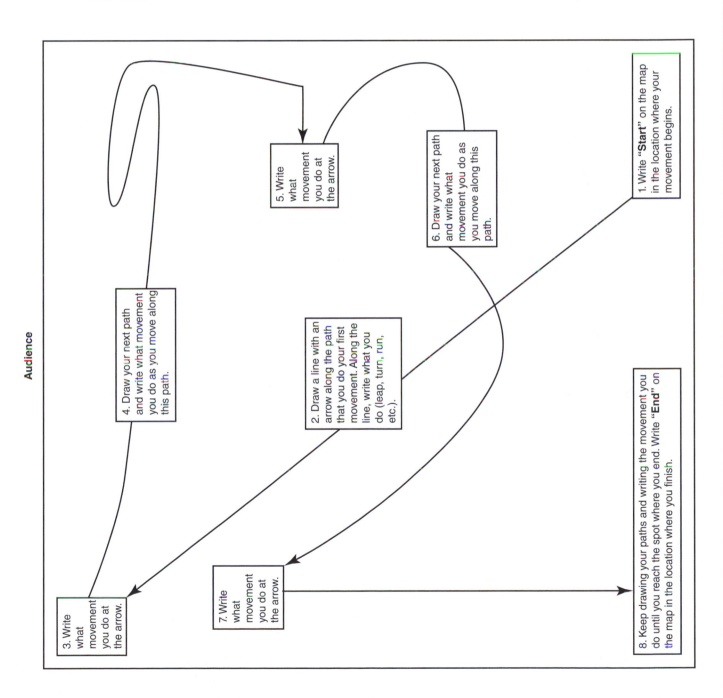

Audience

1. Write **"Start"** on the map in the location where your movement begins.

2. Draw a line with an arrow along the path that you do your first movement. Along the line, write what you do (leap, turn, run, etc.).

3. Write what movement you do at the arrow.

4. Draw your next path and write what movement you do as you move along this path.

5. Write what movement you do at the arrow.

6. Draw your next path and write what movement you do as you move along this path.

7. Write what movement you do at the arrow.

8. Keep drawing your paths and writing the movement you do until you reach the spot where you end. Write **"End"** on the map in the location where you finish.

From J. Fey, 2011, Dance unis for middle school (Champaign, IL: Human Kinetics).

Pathways Map Directions.

movement at the same time. Think about how we did the warm-up for the first few lessons. How did the movement occur? [Students answer: A new group started every 8 counts.] This is called **canon**. How was everyone moving when we warmed up to words? [Students answer: Everyone was doing a different movement.] When you create your project, think about the vocabulary that we learned in each lesson and try to use those ways of moving in your project. [Do a quick review; the words will be up on the wall.]

Okay, it is time to get started. Once you have your group together and have selected your project, come up as a group, and I will assign your group a workstation. Go right to your station and begin work.

Allow students to work in the time remaining. Circulate to monitor and answer questions. Do not tell students how to do the project; they have to figure that out for themselves. If you see that students are pantomiming (acting out), ask them to figure out ways to change the movement so it is not pantomimed. Pantomiming is not part of the project. Remind each group to complete the Daily Contribution Sheet and Pathways Map as they work.

CLOSURE

Do a low-level walk to come over and have a seat. Bring your Pathways Maps, Daily Contribution Sheets, and pencils with you. [Students come over.] We made a lot of progress today. Today was the hard part—getting all the directions and getting started. Tomorrow you will have almost the entire class to work on your project. You will perform your project for the class the following day. [Note: If you want to extend the time for extra days, you will have better results. Do what you know is best for your class.] Tomorrow, at the beginning of class, we will go over the **rubric** for the project. Put your Pathways Map and Daily Contribution Sheet together. One person in each group collects the sheets and brings them to me on your way out. Take your pencil with you and be sure to bring a pencil for the next lesson. [Have paper clips for clipping together the sheets for each group (or student), and put them in the folders you have labeled. That will save time when you hand them out on subsequent days.]

- Did we meet our outcomes for the day?
- Are there any questions?

═══ LESSON 7 ═══

PREPARATION

- Have music ready.
- In the room, have folders with Pathways Maps, Daily Contribution Sheets, and rubrics (available in two-day, three-day, and multiday formats—choose which will be used).
- Have performance space marked off (36 feet wide by 30 feet deep, or 11 m by 9 m, facing audience).
- Post Bring a Pencil sign and have pencils in the room.
- Post signs and outcomes if not previously posted.

LESSON INTRODUCTION

When students enter the room, seat them in lines (squads) facing the audience. Go over outcomes for the lesson.

 ➡ Before we begin working on our projects, we'll look at the Rubric for Improvisation Project. [Pass out Improvisation Project Rubrics and pencils.] As soon as you get your sheet, neatly write your name and class on it. [Students do this.] On performance day, each of you will be scored using this rubric. Notice that how you work each day is part of the scoring. Completion of your Pathways Map and Daily Contribution Sheet is also part of your score. When you worked yesterday, you saw that there were required elements (movements) on your Improvisation Project card. Twenty points are awarded for including all of these elements in your project. *Performance qualities* means that your group obviously practiced the project and performed it seriously, with strong movement, and with a very good attitude. You'll notice that you are also scored on your audience etiquette. That means demonstrating the audience **etiquette** that has been posted since we started our improvisation unit. Does anyone have any questions about the scoring for the project?

Everyone hand in the Improvisation Project Rubric now. [Students do this.] Take a look at the performance space that is marked off with cones (or tape or flags). The project will be performed in this area. As you work today, your group will get to practice in the performance space. We will begin with group 1, then group 2, and so on for the entire class. When it is your group's turn in the performance space, I will play your music. Take your Pathways Map, Daily Contribution Sheet, and pencil to your stations and begin to work.

As you change the music and circulate, notice if the students are able to complete the project by the end of the class. Some groups or classes will do this very quickly. Others may need another day. Extend the working time as long as students are working hard. Also mention that practice outside of class may be necessary so that you can ensure everyone in the group can do the movements well.

CLOSURE

➡ Do a high-level prance to come over and have a seat. One person from each group will collect the Daily Contribution Sheets and Pathways Maps and bring them to me.

- **Option 1.** Because you have worked very hard, and because it looks like all of the groups would benefit from another day of work and practice, we are going to have another class to complete the projects. Remember to practice outside of school. If your group cannot practice together, practice your own part so it will be the best it can be. [In this case, repeat lesson 7 as many times as necessary before moving on to lesson 8.]

- **Option 2**. It looks like everyone has finished the projects. We will all be anxious to watch them tomorrow. Remember that we will expect you to demonstrate audience etiquette for the performances, and everyone will turn in their Pathways Maps and Daily Contribution Sheets for scoring. [In this case, move on to lesson 8 in the next class.]

- Did we meet today's outcomes?

═══ LESSON 8 ═══

PREPARATION

- Have rubrics for each group clipped together.
- Have folders for Pathways Maps and Daily Contribution Sheets ready.
- Have music ready.
- Post Bring a Pencil sign and have pencils in class.
- Post signs and outcomes if not previously posted.
- Post due date for critique.

LESSON INTRODUCTION

When students enter the room, seat them in lines (squads) facing the audience. Review the outcomes for the lesson.

➡ We are all excited about performing our projects and about watching what the other groups have done. You are going to have just a short time to run through your project *once* with music, and then the groups will perform. Go to your stations and work while each group takes a turn in the performance space. Group 1 will be in the performance space first. [Students do this.]

Skip to come to the audience area, turn in your Pathways Map and Daily Contribution Sheet, and have a seat. [The wall that you have been using as audience (downstage) is the audience area where students sit.] Which group would like to go first? [In some classes, everyone will volunteer. In other classes, no one will volunteer. Have a designated order, draw numbers, or use some other method to determine performance order.] What are the expectations for the audience? [Students respond with what has been posted.] Give group _____ your attention. [Read the project card, and then the group performs.]

Complete the Improvisation Project Rubric for each student. The required elements, performance qualities shown, and audience etiquette shown can be evaluated while the group is performing. The day 1, day 2 (and however many days) work and effort can be completed after the last working day. If you decide to have the students work three or more days, use the multiday rubric with space for six days of scoring instead of two days.

At the end of each performance, insist that everyone applaud. Review audience etiquette, if necessary. Ask a question about each performance, such as one of these questions:

➡ • What did you notice that was unusual?
- What movement caught your eye?
- What was interesting about this group's performance?
- Did the group meet the requirements of the project? How do you know this?

Any other questions are fine, as long as they do not single out a particular student's performance.

CLOSURE

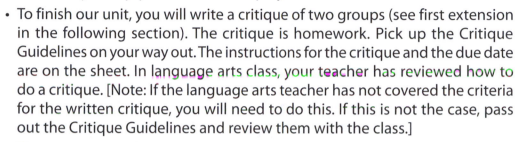 You all did very interesting projects and created movements that were interesting to watch.

- What was most difficult about doing this project?
- What did you enjoy most about the project?
- To finish our unit, you will write a critique of two groups (see first extension in the following section). The critique is homework. Pick up the Critique Guidelines on your way out. The instructions for the critique and the due date are on the sheet. In language arts class, your teacher has reviewed how to do a critique. [Note: If the language arts teacher has not covered the criteria for the written critique, you will need to do this. If this is not the case, pass out the Critique Guidelines and review them with the class.]
- The critiques are due on _____.

EXTENSION

- Videotape the performances and have students watch themselves before writing their critiques.
- Invite parents, other teachers, the principal, and others to see the performances.
- Use the performances for other school and community events.
- Select two groups whose movement is similar and have them perform for the class one after the other; the second group enters as the first group exits.
- Have the groups perform without music and ask the audience how that changed what they saw.

UNIT TWO

DANCE FOR ATHLETES

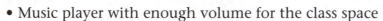

1

INTRODUCTION
AND WARM-UP

OUTCOMES

- Students will learn correct technique for a variety of warm-up exercises.
- Students will identify fitness components that improve as the result of a variety of warm-up exercises.
- Students will practice executing the warm-up correctly to music.

NATIONAL DANCE STANDARDS

- Identifying and demonstrating movement elements and skills in performing dance
- Making connections between dance and healthful living
- Making connections between dance and other disciplines

MATERIALS

- Music player with enough volume for the class space

- Music with steady fast beat and appropriate words (accompanying CD or see suggestions on page xxiii)
- Notebooks (students supply their own, or you can provide folders for each student)

- Stage directions signs

- Handouts: Dance for Athletes Warm-Up Chart, Rules for Safe Stretching, Physical Fitness Definitions, Homework Essay, Homework Essay Rubric

PREPARATION

- Post the outcomes for the lesson.

- Post the vocabulary for the lesson.

- Laminate signs for stage right, stage left, upstage, downstage, and audience. Put signs on walls in class space using Stage Directions Diagram (see page 48) as a guide.
- Enlarge Dance for Athletes Warm-Up Chart and post or project chart onto the audience wall so that students can easily see it.

DANCE FOR ATHLETES WARM-UP CHART

Turn on music, count "5, 6, 7, 8," and start exercise on count 1.

Exercise	Counts	Body parts	Compone...
Roll down and up 2 times	8 fast counts down, 8 fast counts up (32 total counts)	Spine	Flexibility, injury prev...
Head circle 8, head...	16 f...		

RULES FOR SAFE STRETCHING

- Stretch *after* warming up.
- Always use proper technique for each stretch.
- Do not bounce.
- Hold stretch for 30 seconds.
- Relax while stretching.

PHYSICAL FITNESS DEFINITIONS

WHAT IS PHYSICAL FITNESS?

Physical fitness is the ability of the whole body (including muscles, skeleton, heart, and all other body parts) to work together efficiently. A physically fit body is able to do the most work with the least amount of effort. To develop and maintain physical fitness, a person must exercise regularly.

CRITIQUE GUIDELINES

Critique—A critique is an analysis of what one sees in a perfor... the criteria for the performance. It is not a criticism, althou... some of the criteria were not met and why.

Each student will write a critique of two of the group... critique will be of the whole group, not of any individual... The critique will meet these guidelines:

- The critique will be written or typed in good form...
- Use 12-point font for typed work.
- The critique will be hand written or printed in bl...
- Handwriting must be neat and legible.
- The critique will contain paragraphs, correct sp... complete sentences, and correct punctuation.
- The critique will have student's name, date, an... corner of the first page.
- The critique will be titled "___ ... will be in the center of the top line of the firs...
- The critique will begin with an introduction...
- The critique will contain paragraphs abou... analyzed. These paragraphs will discuss the... the choreography, the performance qualities... for improvement, if any. Explain what you... are saying in the critique is true. Be sure... which you are writing.
- The critique will end with a summary.
- The critique will be turned in on the day...

Critique due date: _____

HOMEWORK ESSAY RUBRIC

Name_____ Class_____

Item	Possible points	Points earned
Venn diagram (neat and legible)	10	
Essay: introduction	15	
Essay: similarities	15	
Essay: differences	15	
	15	

HOMEWORK ESSAY

DANCERS AND ATHLETES: SIMILAR AND DIFFERENT

Use a Venn di... to show the similarities and differences between dancers ...nn diagram should be neat and legible. ...te the Venn diagram, write an essay titled "Dancers and ...t." The title should be at the top of the page. Put ...class period in the upper-right corner of the page. ...th an introduction, contain paragraphs about the ...dancers and athletes, explain how dance ...formance, explain how sports can help

...ct spelling, correct grammar, complete

...per or type the essay. Use black ink only. ...le. Use 12-point font for typed work.

AUDIENCE

From J. Fey, 2011, *Dance units for middle school* (Champaign, IL: Human Kinetics).

 • Write due dates on Homework Essay handout before running it off.

 • Run off enough Dance for Athletes Warm-Up Charts, Rules for Safe Stretching, Physical Fitness Definitions, Homework Essay handouts, and Homework Essay Rubrics for all students.

 • Give the Critique Guidelines sheet to the language arts teachers, and ask them to go over it with students as part of the language arts class. Do this before or at the beginning of the unit (or at the beginning of the school year) so there is plenty of time to incorporate this into the language arts class.

• If using the accompanying DVD to demonstrate technique, have it ready.

VOCABULARY

- roll down and roll up
- head circle
- transition
- abdominals (abs)
- iliopsoas
- hamstrings
- biceps
- triceps
- quadriceps
- hip flexor
- gastrocnemius
- Achilles tendon
- soleus

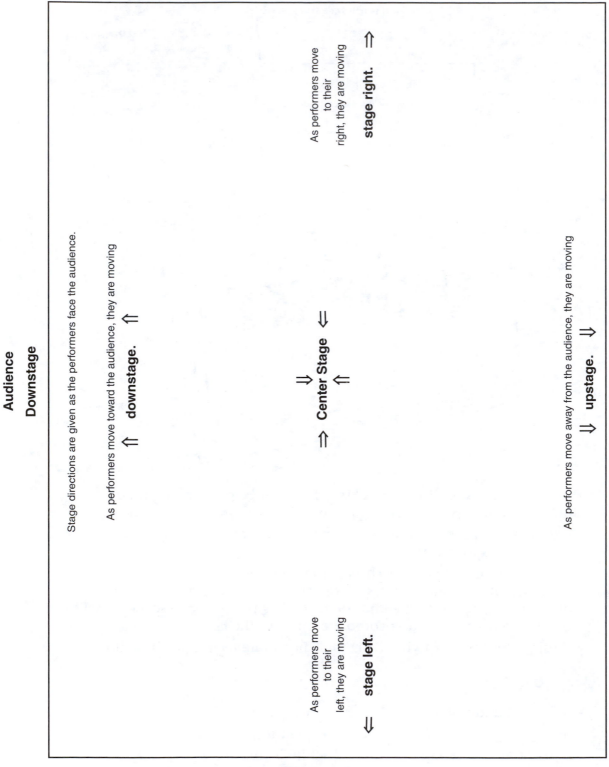

Stage Directions Diagram.

48

LESSON INTRODUCTION

When students enter the room, seat them in their lines (squads) facing the wall chosen for audience and downstage. Make sure lines are spread out and take up the whole class space so students can lie down front to back and side to side without touching each other. Consider putting warm-up marks on the floor with tape if your students are not good at staying in their spaces.

Review the outcomes for the lesson.

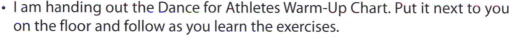 We are beginning our unit on dance for athletes. Some high schools have a course on dance for athletes, for which students receive physical education or fine arts credit. Many top-notch college athletic programs require all of their athletes to take dance because dance training helps athletes perform better.

Most athletic training works the large muscle groups in the body. Can you name some large muscle groups? [Let students respond: quadriceps, hamstrings, back, shoulders.] Dance training, in addition to working large muscle groups, isolates the smaller muscles in the body. The smaller muscles often are not used very much, and isolating them makes it easier for athletes to use their smaller muscles. Using the smaller muscles improves balance, agility, power, speed, timing, coordination, footwork, and jumping, in addition to flexibility, muscular strength, and endurance. This is why athletes who use dance as part of their training improve their abilities. Can you name some well-known athletes who take dance? [Herschel Walker performed with Houston Ballet, gymnasts and figure skaters study dance, University of Iowa wrestlers take dance, Wilt Chamberlain took ballet.]

Now we will learn our warm-up for dance for athletes.

 • I am handing out the Dance for Athletes Warm-Up Chart. Put it next to you on the floor and follow as you learn the exercises.

 • Next you are receiving Rules for Safe Stretching. We'll go over them. [Do this.] Be sure to think about and use these rules as you do the warm-up.

• Both handouts go into your notebooks (or folders) at the end of class.

 • I will demonstrate correct technique one exercise at a time (or use the accompanying DVD to demonstrate).

• We will then perform each exercise while I watch and count immediately after each demonstration.

• We will correct technique immediately and repeat the exercise, if necessary.

• Note that the counts are listed by each exercise on the Dance for Athletes Warm-Up Chart.

• All counts are the fast beats of the music.

Teach students the warm-up using these coaching cues:

Roll Down and Up

8 fast counts down, 8 fast counts up, done twice, total of 32 counts

 • Feet are parallel and shoulder-width apart.

• Weight is on both feet and mostly on the balls of the feet the whole time.

- Head leads the way down, upper back follows, then lower back, then butt.
- Arms, shoulders, and neck are relaxed the whole time.
- No pushing or straining; gravity does the work.
- Butt leads the way up, then lower back, then upper back, then neck, then head.
- Abdominal muscles pull you up.
- Use smooth and continuous movement down and up.
- Look on your chart. What body part are we working on? [Spine.]
- What fitness components? [Flexibility, balance, injury prevention.]
- Now we will roll down and up as listed on the warm-up chart. Count silently to yourself as I count. [Do this with students several times, giving corrections. Do 8 fast counts down, 8 fast counts up, done twice, for a total of 32 counts.]

Head Circle Right, Head Circle Left
16 fast counts for each head circle, total of 32 counts

- Start by looking to the right, then bring chin to chest, then look left, then look up at ceiling, then look right, then chin to chest, and finish looking left. This is a head circle to the **right.**
- Reverse by looking to the left, chin to chest, and so on, and ending up looking right. This is a head circle to the **left.**
- Totally relax the neck, shoulders, and arms.
- Do not crank the head back; simply look up to the ceiling.
- Feet are parallel and shoulder-width apart.
- Abdominals are tight the whole time.
- Look on your chart. What body part are we working on? [Neck.]
- What fitness components? [Flexibility, injury prevention.]
- Now we will do head circles right and left as listed on the warm-up sheet. Count silently to yourself as I count. [Do this with students several times, giving corrections. Do 16 fast counts for each head circle, for a total of 32 counts.]

2-Count Jumping Jacks
16 jumping jacks, 2 fast counts each, total of 32 counts

- Feet jump apart as hands meet overhead.
- Extend the arms long.
- Feet jump together as hands come down to sides.
- Do not slap sides.
- Keep abdominals tight the whole time.
- Keep weight on balls of feet.
- Look on your chart. What body parts are we working on? [Full body.]

- What fitness components? [Cardiorespiratory endurance.]
- Now we will do jumping jacks as listed on the warm-up sheet. Count silently to yourself as I count. [Do this with students and give corrections. Do 16 jumping jacks, 2 fast counts each, for a total of 32 counts.]

Reach Overhead
Hold for 32 fast counts

- Feet are parallel and shoulder-width apart.
- Do not arch the back.
- Abdominals are tight.
- Look up at hands.
- Arms should be as long as possible.
- Look on your chart. What body parts are we working on? [Back, shoulders.]
- What fitness component? [Flexibility.]
- Now we will reach overhead as listed on the warm-up sheet. Count silently to yourself as I count. [Do this with students and give corrections. Hold for 32 fast counts.]

Reach Back
Hold for 32 fast counts

- Feet are parallel and shoulder-width apart.
- Do not arch the back.
- Abdominals are tight.
- Lift arms as high as possible in back while standing up straight.
- Look on your chart. What body parts are we working on? [Shoulders, chest.]
- What fitness component? [Flexibility.]
- Now we will reach back as listed on the warm-up sheet. Count silently to yourself as I count. [Do this with students and give corrections. Hold for 32 fast counts.]

Transition to Floor
8 fast counts

- Turn and face stage right.
- Quickly lie down and get into crunch position. [Note: If students have had the improvisation unit, they know how to fall.]
- You will be sideways to the audience with your feet toward stage right so that you can see me and I can monitor your technique.
- Now we will transition to floor as listed on the warm-up sheet. Count silently to yourself as I count. [Do this with students and give corrections. Do it in 8 fast counts.]

Crunches

32 crunches, 2 fast counts each, total of 64 counts

Note: Some students might not be able to do all of the crunches the first time they try it. Encourage students to work up to doing 32 crunches (2 fast counts each, for a total of 64 counts). If any student needs to take a break during the 32, tell the student to hold the navel down to the floor to at least activate the abs while resting. **Do not decrease the number of crunches.**

- Feet are shoulder-width apart.
- Knees are bent, and feet are flat on floor.
- Hands are either at sides or on the base of the skull, not on the neck; elbows should be held still and not "flap," which pulls on the neck and strains the neck and upper back.
- Chin is tucked to chest gently to help round the back.
- Curl up until shoulder blades are off the floor—no higher.
- Curl back down.
- The back stays rounded the entire time—no flat backs.
- The navel stays "snapped" to the floor the entire time.
- Look on your chart. What body part are we working on? [Upper abs.]
- What fitness component? [Muscular strength.]
- Now we will do crunches as listed on the warm-up sheet. Count silently to yourself as I count. [Do this with students and give corrections. Do 32 crunches, 2 fast counts each, for a total of 64 counts.]

Oblique Crunches

16 right and 16 left, 2 fast counts each, total of 64 counts

Note: Some students may not be able to do all of the crunches the first time they try it. Encourage students to work up to doing 32 (16 right side and then 16 left side, 2 fast counts each, total of 64 counts). If any student needs to take a break during the 32, have him or her hold the navel down to the floor to at least activate the abs while resting. **Do not decrease the number of crunches.**

- Use the same position and rules as for crunches.
- Curl up with a twist to the opposite knee (toward 2 o'clock for right and toward 10 o'clock for left) until the lower shoulder blade is just off the floor.
- Keep the back of both hips flat on the floor.
- Keep the navel "snapped."
- Look on your chart. What body part are we working on? [Oblique abs.]
- What fitness component? [Muscular strength.]
- Now we will do oblique crunches as listed on the warm-up sheet. Count silently to yourself as I count. [Do this with students and give corrections. Do 16 right and 16 left, 2 fast counts each, for a total of 64 counts.]

Leg-Out Crunches
16 right and 16 left, 2 fast counts each, total of 64 counts

Note: Butt-ups may be substituted for leg-out crunches. If butt-ups are done, the legs are up off the floor at 90 degrees and crossed at the ankles with knees slightly bent. The legs do not move. The butt is lifted off the floor only 1 inch. The upper body should not be involved in the movement.

Note: Some students may not be able to do all of the crunches the first time they try it (16 right and 16 left, 2 fast counts each, total of 64 counts). Encourage students to work up to doing 32. If any student needs to take a break during the 32, have him or her hold the navel down to the floor to at least activate the abs while resting. **Do not decrease the number of crunches.**

- Use the same rules as for crunches.
- One knee is bent, and the other leg is held straight out and off the floor *only* about 6 inches, no higher.
- Curl up until both shoulder blades are just off the floor, just as in crunches.
- Look on your chart. What body part are we working on? [Lower abs.]
- What fitness component? [Muscular strength.]
- Now we will do leg-out crunches as listed on the warm-up sheet. Count silently to yourself as I count. [Do this with students and give corrections. Do 16 right and 16 left, 2 fast counts each, for a total of 64 counts.]

Hug Knees to Chest
Hold for 32 fast counts

- Relax, lie on back, and hug knees to chest.
- Make sure the back of the hips and shoulder blades are on the floor.
- The arms do the work—everything else is relaxed. This relieves any tension put on the back during crunches and prevents injury.
- Look on your chart. What body part are we working on? [Back.]
- What fitness component? [Injury prevention.]
- Now we will hug knees to chest as listed on the warm-up sheet. Count silently to yourself as I count. [Do this with students and give corrections. Hold for 32 fast counts.]

Transition to Cobra
8 fast counts

- Stretch out straight lying on back.
- Log roll downstage (toward audience) to belly.
- Put hands under shoulders.
- Use arms to push to cobra position.
- Now we will transition to cobra as listed on the warm-up sheet. Count silently to yourself as I count. [Do this with students and give corrections. Do this in 8 fast counts.]

Cobra Stretch
Hold for 32 fast counts

Note: Some students will not be able to straighten their arms without lifting their hips off the floor.

- Hands are placed under shoulders.
- The entire body is relaxed.
- Hips remain on floor.
- The weight is on the arms.
- Think of the spine hanging down through (or sagging between) the shoulders.
- You should feel this in the front of the ribs only, not the back.
- Look on your chart. What body part are we working on? [Iliopsoas.]
- What fitness component? [Flexibility.]
- Now we will do cobra stretch as listed on the warm-up sheet. Count silently to yourself as I count. [Do this with students and give corrections. Hold for 32 fast counts.]

Ankle Grab
Hold for 32 fast counts

Note: This is a safer way to stretch the quads than the standing stretch. In the standing stretch, people often are not aligned properly and twist their knees and hips.

- Start by lying on your belly.
- Knees are *together*.
- Reach back to hold ankles or feet and pull the heels toward the butt.

Note: Some students will not be able to grab ankles or feet. They can grab the backs of their shoes or socks. Some students will be so tight that they can grab only one leg at a time. Those students should work one leg for 16 counts and the other leg for 16 counts and work on this stretch at home. Students who are already flexible will need to hold farther up their shins in order to feel a stretch.

- Look on your chart. What body part are we working on? [Quadriceps.]
- What fitness component? [Flexibility.]
- Now we will do ankle grab as listed on the warm-up sheet. Count silently to yourself as I count. [Do this with students and give corrections. Hold for 32 fast counts.]

Transition to Triangle
8 fast counts

- Stretch out straight on belly.
- Put hands under shoulders and dig toes into floor.

- Walk hands in toward feet to get into triangle position.
- Now we will transition to triangle as listed on the warm-up sheet. Count silently to yourself as I count. [Do this with students and give corrections. Do it in 8 fast counts.]

Triangle Push-Ups

4 push-ups of 8 fast counts down and 8 fast counts up, total of 64 counts

Note: Many students will only be able to hold the triangle at first; bending the arms will come with practice. Encourage them to bend just a little and hold, then bend more and more until they can do the push-up. They should work toward 4 push-ups of 8 fast counts down and 8 fast counts up (total of 64 counts).

- The butt should be at the top of the triangle.
- Knees are straight.
- Belly is tight.
- Feet are in parallel second position, and heels may come up off the floor.
- Triangle shape is maintained throughout the push-up.
- Shoulders are directly over hands.
- Use slow, continuous movement all the way down, then all the way up.
- Even holding the triangle puts a lot of weight on the arms.
- Look on your chart. What body parts are we working on? [Biceps, triceps.]
- What fitness component? [Muscular strength.]
- Now we will do triangle push-ups as listed on the warm-up sheet. Count silently to yourself as I count. [Do this with students and give corrections. Do it in 64 fast counts.]

Low Lunge Right and Left

Right and left, hold for 32 fast counts on each side

- The weight is on the arms and back foot, not the knee.
- The angle of the front knee should be 90 degrees or greater to protect the knee.
- Hands are inside the knee.
- The back leg is straight.
- Try to have a straight line between your back foot and your head.
- Relax the neck and head—do not look out at the horizon.
- Gravity will take the weight down and stretch the hip flexor.
- After holding 32 fast counts, change knees quickly. Hold for 32 fast counts on each side.
- Look on your chart. What body part are we working on? [Hip flexor.]
- What fitness component? [Flexibility.]
- Now we will do low lunge right and left as listed on the warm-up sheet. Count silently to yourself as I count. [Do this with students and give corrections. Hold for 32 fast counts on each side.]

Mountain Climbers

16 repetitions, 1 fast count each, total of 16 fast counts

- These are really fast!
- Both feet touch the floor on each change of position.
- Bring the knees as close to the chest as possible.
- The body should be flat from the head to the foot.
- Weight is on the arms during the exchange of feet.
- Look on your chart. What body parts are we working on? [Hip flexor, abs.]
- What fitness components? [Muscular strength and endurance, agility.]
- Now we will do mountain climbers as listed on the warm-up sheet. Count silently to yourself as I count. [Do this with students and give corrections. Do 16, 1 fast count each, for a total of 16 fast counts.]

Transition to Butterfly

8 fast counts

- Sit up tall, facing audience. Soles of feet are together.
- Place hands on ankles.
- Now we will transition to butterfly as listed on the warm-up sheet. Count silently to yourself as I count. [Do this with students and give corrections. Do it in 8 fast counts.]

Butterfly Stretch

Hold for 32 fast counts

Note: Some inflexible students will also feel this in the neck and upper back. These students need to relax by gently shaking their heads yes and no while holding the stretch.

- Hold the ankles, *never* the toes. Holding the toes overstretches the outsides of the feet and ankles and makes it easier to roll over the foot. It also makes you more prone to ankle injury.
- Relax the entire body.
- Curl forward, head first, and hold.
- At the end of the stretch, curl back up, lower back first, head last.
- You should feel this stretch in the groin and back.
- Do not strain or push; gravity does the work.
- Look on your chart. What body parts are we working on? [Groin, back.]
- What fitness component? [Flexibility.]
- Now we will do the butterfly stretch as listed on the warm-up sheet. Count silently to yourself as I count. [Do this with students and give corrections. Hold for 32 fast counts.]

Pike Stretch
Hold for 32 fast counts

Note: Some inflexible students will only be able to put the chin on the chest. They might also need to bend the knees to sit up straight to do this. Encourage practice. Students can check to see if their heads are relaxed by shaking their heads yes and no while holding the stretch.

- We have to change from butterfly to pike on the count of 1—it is very quick.
- Arms, shoulders, and head are relaxed (put hands on thighs).
- Sit up straight with straight knees (see previous note).
- Feet are relaxed (students who are flexible can flex the feet for a better stretch).
- Curl down, head first, and hold.
- Relax totally.
- Curl up, starting with the lower back.
- You should feel the stretch from the heels to the head along the back.
- Do not strain or push; gravity does the work.
- Look on your chart. What body parts are we working on? [Back, hamstrings.]
- What fitness component? [Flexibility.]
- Now we will do the pike stretch as listed on the warm-up sheet. Count silently to yourself as I count. [Do this with students and give corrections. Hold for 32 fast counts.]

V-Sit (Straddle)
Hold for 32 fast counts

Note: Some inflexible students will not even be able to sit in a straddle. They can bend their knees and make the V smaller so they can curl the head down a little. Encourage them to hang out and relax. It will improve with practice.

- We have to change from pike to straddle on the count of 1—it is very quick.
- Arms, shoulders, and head are relaxed.
- Knees and toes face up toward the ceiling the whole time.
- Feet are relaxed (students who are flexible can flex the feet for a better stretch).
- Curl down, head first, and hold.
- Relax totally.
- Curl up, starting with lower back.
- Do not strain or push; gravity does the work.
- Look on your chart. What body parts are we working on? [Groin, back, hamstrings.]
- What fitness component? [Flexibility.]
- Now we will do the straddle stretch as listed on the warm-up sheet. Count silently to yourself as I count. [Do this with students and give corrections. Hold for 32 fast counts.]

Transition to Inverted Stretch
8 fast counts

- In straddle stretch, slide legs together on counts 1, 2.
- Pull knees to chest on counts 3, 4.
- Place hands behind butt and keep head down.
- Use arms to push to the feet. Stay tucked in a ball on counts 5, 6.
- Let head and arms hang relaxed and straighten knees on counts 7, 8.
- We are now in inverted stretch position.
- Now we will transition to inverted stretch as listed on the warm-up sheet. Count silently to yourself as I count. [Do this with students and give corrections. Do it in 8 fast counts.]

Inverted Stretch
Hold for 32 fast counts

Note: Students can check to see if the head is relaxed by shaking the head yes and no while holding the stretch.

- Feet are shoulder-width apart and parallel (parallel first position).
- Hang with relaxed head, arms, and shoulders.
- Weight is mostly on balls of feet.
- Do not hyperextend knees.
- You should feel the stretch from the head to heel along the back.
- Look on your chart. What body parts are we working on? [Back, hamstrings.]
- What fitness components? [Flexibility, balance.]
- Now we will do inverted stretch as listed on the warm-up sheet. Count silently to yourself as I count. [Do this with students and give corrections. Hold for 32 fast counts.]

Roll Up
8 fast counts

- Arms, shoulders, and neck are relaxed the whole time.
- Do not push or strain; gravity does the work.
- Butt leads the way up, then lower back, then upper back, then neck, then head.
- Abdominal muscles pull you up.
- Use smooth and continuous movement up.
- Look on your chart. What body part are we working on? [Spine.]
- What fitness components? [Alignment, injury prevention, balance.]
- Now we will roll up as listed on the warm-up chart. Count silently to yourself as I count. [Do this with students several times, giving corrections. Do it in 8 fast counts up.]

Parallel Lunges

Hold for 32 fast counts with straight left leg, then 32 fast counts with bent left knee (64 counts total for left), then repeat whole series on right

Right foot steps forward in lunge while left knee stays straight for 32 counts. Then left knee bends and left heel lifts about an inch for 32 counts. Change legs and left foot steps forward in lunge while right knee stays straight for 32 counts. Then right knee bends and right heel lifts about an inch for 32 counts. Hold for total of 64 counts on each leg.

Note: Students will want to turn out the back foot. A turned-out back foot does not allow for the correct stretch, and it twists the hip, knee, and ankle into an unsafe position.

- Start with feet parallel and at least shoulder-width apart.
- We will do the lunges with the right foot forward, then quickly change to left foot forward.
- Step right foot straight forward into a lunge (fourth position parallel).
- Abdominals are tight the whole time.
- Head is up, and back is not arched.
- Using a straight back leg with weight on the front foot, push the heel down and hold for 32 counts.
- Then bend the back knee slightly and lift the heel an inch if needed without changing body position.
- Look at your chart. What body parts are we working on with a straight back knee? [Gastrocnemius and Achilles tendon.]
- What body part are we working on with a bent back knee? [Soleus.]
- What fitness component? [Flexibility.]
- Now we will do parallel lunge as listed on the warm-up chart. Count silently to yourself as I count. [Do this slowly with students and give corrections. Hold for 32 fast counts with straight leg, then 32 fast counts with bent knee. Do right and left parallel lunges.]

You have done a good job learning the movements for our warm-up. It might seem that the warm-up is long. Actually, once we do it to music without any breaks, it is not long at all. Does anyone have any questions about the warm-up technique? [Answer any questions.]

Now we will do the warm-up to music. We will make mistakes at first. That's okay; just keep trying. You are in charge of your own warm-up. At first, some of the warm-up might be hard for you, but the goal is to work on it until you are able to do all parts correctly and completely. If you make a mistake, keep going and don't worry. Practice makes perfect! Your goal is to be ready for the next exercise so you can start each new exercise on the count of 1. [Practice the whole warm-up a couple of times.]

CLOSURE

 Hand out the Homework Essay and Homework Essay Rubric handouts. Go over the assignment. Note the due date (which should be after the unit is over so students have the information they need in order to write the essay) for the Venn diagram and the essay. Explain that students will get the information they need for the essay as they pay attention during each lesson in class, so they should not start writing right away.

- Did you accomplish the outcomes for the lesson?
- What was hard and what was easy?
- For the next class, you will need to memorize the order of the warm-up.
- I expect to see a big improvement during each class!
- Practice difficult parts of the warm-up at home.
- Let's go over the handout of definitions of physical fitness. [Hand out Physical Fitness Definitions.] You will need to know the components of physical fitness and be able to explain them.
- Put your Warm-Up Chart, Rules for Safe Stretching, and Physical Fitness Definitions in your notebooks or folders.
- Tomorrow you will learn plyometrics. Your assignment before class tomorrow is to find out the definition of plyometrics.

EXTENSION

- Ask for students (11) to volunteer to make posters for each of the 11 components of physical fitness (from the Physical Fitness Definitions handout) and put the posters up on the wall.
- Ask for students (20) to volunteer to make posters of each of the 20 exercises in the warm-up (showing correct technique) and put the posters up on the wall. The 20 exercises do not include the transitions.

NOTE FOR TEACHERS

Depending on the length of the class, students' experience with exercise technique, the physical fitness and stamina of the class, and how many questions and corrections are needed, this lesson could take several classes before students do the movements correctly.

2

PLYOMETRICS

OUTCOMES

- Students will learn the definition of plyometrics.
- Students will learn stage directions.
- Students will learn the definition of canon.
- Students will learn how to perform movement in canon.
- Students will practice correct technique for locomotor movements.

NATIONAL DANCE STANDARDS

- Identifying and demonstrating movement elements and skills in performing dance
- Making connections between dance and healthful living
- Making connections between dance and other disciplines

MATERIALS

- Music player with enough volume for class space
 - Music with fast, steady beat and appropriate words (accompanying CD or see suggestions on page xxiii)
 - Handouts: Plyometrics, Stage Directions Diagram, Origin of Stage Directions
- Cones or tape to mark off starting and stopping points for plyometrics
 - DVD of plyometric skills

PREPARATION

 - Post the outcomes for the lesson.
 - Post the vocabulary for the lesson.
 - Stage signs should be up from lesson 1.
- Run off enough handouts of Plyometrics, Stage Directions Diagram, and Origin of Stage Directions for each student.
- Decide the starting and ending spots (stage right and stage left) for plyometrics. Use cones, tape, or flags to identify where you want each line to stand.
 - Project Warm-Up Chart on audience wall (or post enlarged chart).
- If using the DVD to demonstrate plyometric skills, have it set up and ready.

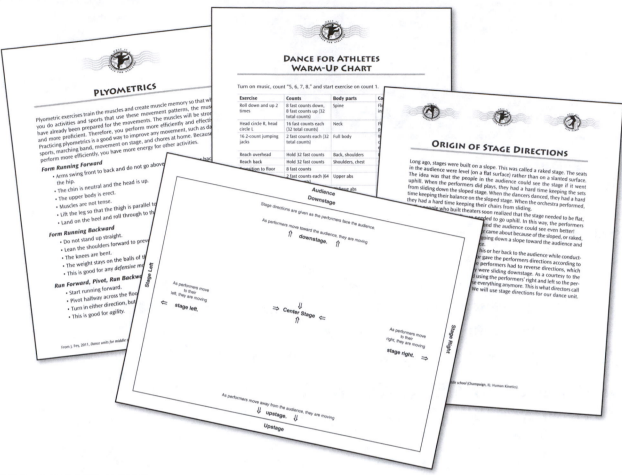

VOCABULARY

- plyometrics
- canon
- locomotor
- over
- back
- slide

- grapevine
- jog
- hop
- leap
- skip
- sprint

Note that some of the vocabulary terms are defined in the Plyometrics handout rather than the lesson.

LESSON INTRODUCTION

When students enter the room, seat them in their lines (squads) facing the audience. Be sure they are spaced far enough apart to do the warm-up without touching each other. Each student will need about a 10-foot square space.

Audience

X X X X X X
X X X X X X
X X X X X X
X X X X X X
X X X X X X

Review the outcomes for the lesson.

Have you practiced the warm-up from lesson 1? I expect to see much improvement today and even more improvement for lesson 3.

After we do the warm-up, we will learn plyometrics. Now let's do our warm-up. Remember, you are responsible for your own warm-up, for correct technique, for having the warm-up memorized, and for executing it on the correct counts. [Complete the warm-up from lesson 1. Continually monitor technique and give corrections.]

Have a seat. Dance is done on a stage. You might have noticed signs on the walls that mark upstage, downstage (or audience), stage left, and stage right. This is how those stage directions came about. [Read the Origin of Stage Directions handout. Consider having four students each read a paragraph from the handout.] At the end of class you will receive a Stage Directions Diagram and Origin of Stage Directions handout to put in your notebook.

We will now move our lines (squads) to the position for plyometrics. You will be seated just as you are now, except that you will be on the stage-left side of the space facing the stage-right wall of the room and you will be close to each other. [Seat students in their lines (squads) facing stage right as follows (example shows a class of 30 divided into 5 lines of 6 students each, facing stage right):

Audience

X X X X X X

X X X X X X

X X X X X X

X X X X X X

X X X X X X

Make the distance between lines as large as the space permits.

We will do plyometrics in canon. **Canon** means that one group begins, then another group, then another group. It's like "Row, Row, Row Your Boat." It's important that each group begin at the right time, just like when singing in canon. We will do **locomotor**, or traveling, movements in canon.

Did anyone find the definition of plyometrics? [Call on students for answers.] **Plyometrics** is a type of exercise training that produces fast, powerful movements and improves the functioning of the nervous system, generally for the purpose of improving performance in sports. Plyometric movements involve loading a muscle and then contracting it in rapid sequence. This type of exercise uses the strength, elasticity, and innervation of muscle and surrounding tissues to jump higher, run faster, throw farther, or hit harder, depending on your training goal. Plyometrics increases the speed or force of muscular contractions, providing explosiveness for a variety of sport-specific activities. By doing the movements correctly and repeatedly, you create movement memory in your brain, which applies to the action in your muscles, much like the memory in a computer. Each time you practice the movement correctly, the movement improves, and the brain replaces the old memory with the improved memory. In this way, athletes make their movement much more efficient. Who else might benefit from this kind of training? [Students answer: dancers, anyone doing repetitive chores (vacuuming), plumbers, factory workers, surgeons, anyone whose job involves quick action of muscles and repeated movements.]

I will explain the method for going across the floor with music. I will start the movement with "5, 6, 7, 8." From stage left, you will start on your right foot on the count of 1. From stage right, you will start on your left foot on the count of 1. The first row will begin and do the movement all the way across the floor. [Show students their rows.] The second row will be counting and will begin 8 counts after the first row. The third row will be counting and will begin 8 counts after the second row. Each group always begins their movement on the count of 1, and all steps are on the beat of the music. This pattern will continue until all groups have moved across the floor. As each row finishes their movement, they will line up to come back across the floor. Everyone is to stay in their line at all times and count at all times. Do you have any questions about how we move across the floor? [Review and ask questions to make sure students understand. It might be necessary to do a quick demonstration.]

We will begin with walking on the beat. Everyone is to softly count sets of 8 out loud while they are waiting their turn and while they walk. First we will start with the right foot and walk **over**, which means from stage left to stage right. When all have finished and are lined up on the stage-right side, I will call out, "5, 6, 7, 8," and the first group begins walking back, starting with the left foot. **Back** means from stage right to stage left. It is everyone's responsibility to count and have their row come in on the count of 1 every set of 8 counts. We will practice until we can do this. [Students do this. They might need to practice several times before each group automatically comes in every 8 counts. Note: It is important that the students be able to count and come in on time. If you are counting all the time, you cannot give corrections.]

Now that we understand how to come in on the count, we will do our plyometrics. Some of the skills might be difficult for you to do all the way across the class space. Do as much as you can, then keep walking across, and if you can start the skill again after walking several steps, start it again. The idea is to work up to doing all of the skills all the way across the space with good technique. This will improve physical fitness in addition to improving skills. Always try your best! I will demonstrate (or the DVD will demonstrate) each plyometric movement, then the class will do it. Remember to always count and begin each movement on the correct foot on count 1.

- Use the cues on the Plyometrics handout (and DVD) to teach each of the skills. Remind students to begin with the right foot on the stage-left side before you call out, "5, 6, 7, 8." Remind students to begin with the left foot on the stage-right side before you call out, "5, 6, 7, 8."

- One at a time, demonstrate correct technique for each plyometric skill, then have students count and do that skill.

- Correct technique immediately.

- Repeat a skill if needed.

- Complete all of the various plyometric skills.

- Be sure to cite the fitness component for each skill (from the Plyometrics handout).

Do a **slide** over and sit in your warm-up spots facing the audience. [Students do this.] The warm-up and plyometrics do not take long at all once you learn them. I will give coaching cues in each lesson, and I expect you to listen to the cues and make the corrections. Everyone in our class should watch each other carefully and notice the corrections being made. We learn how to be better movers by watching, listening, practicing, and correcting.

CLOSURE

- Did we meet all of our outcomes for today? If not, why not?
- What was hard and what was easy? [Possible answers are counting, staying on the beat, using the correct foot.]
- What do we need to work on to be better? [Follow directions, count, listen, concentrate.]
- Let's look at the Plyometrics handout. [Hand out the Plyometrics handout. Review the definitions and review physical fitness components for each skill.]
- Let's go over the definitions of physical fitness. [Hand out Physical Fitness Definitions and go over definitions.]
- Let's review the stage directions. [Hand out Stage Directions Diagram and Origin of Stage Directions.]
- Put all of the handouts in your notebooks (or folders to be kept in the class).
- Tomorrow, after your warm-up and plyometrics, you will work on skill-related components of fitness.
- Name the skill-related components of physical fitness. [Students can look at their handouts.]
- How do you improve your skills? [Practice.] I encourage you to practice outside of class.
- Good class!

EXTENSION

- Ask for student volunteers to make posters of the plyometric skills to be put on the wall.
- Ask students to make up their own plyometric skill and teach it to the class.

NOTE TO TEACHERS

As with other lessons, depending on class length and students' ability, this lesson might take more than one class period. Students who are not reasonably physically fit might not be able to do all of the skills all the way across the space. Encourage practice outside of class and assure them that they will improve their fitness by doing this unit.

3 & 4

SKILL-RELATED FITNESS COMPONENTS

OUTCOMES

- Students will learn the correct technique for a variety of movements.
- Students will associate movements with skill-related fitness components.
- Students will analyze personal movement.
- Students will practice a variety of movement combinations.

NATIONAL DANCE STANDARDS

- Identifying and demonstrating movement elements and skills in performing dance
- Applying and demonstrating critical-thinking and creative-thinking skills in dance
- Making connections between dance and healthful living
- Making connections between dance and other disciplines

MATERIALS

- Music player with enough volume for class space
- Music with fast, steady beat and appropriate words (accompanying CD or see suggestions on page xxiii)
- Whistle or device that makes a sound loud enough for everyone to hear in the space

PREPARATION

- Post the outcomes for the lessons.

- Post the vocabulary for the lessons.
- Decide which CD tracks will work best for each movement combination, and note the choices.

- Stage signs should be on the walls from lesson 1 and lesson 2.

- Post or project Warm-Up Chart on audience wall.
- Have the Plyometrics handout on hand ready to use.

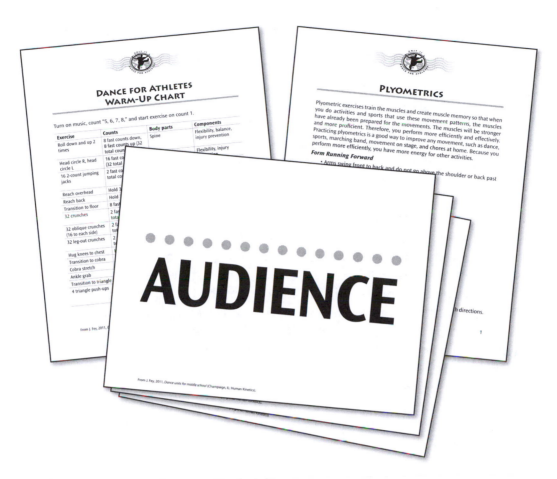

VOCABULARY

- reaction time
- balance
- coordination
- isolations
- diaphragm
- changing weight
- jump turn
- demi-plié

- three-step turn
- paddle turn
- step
- touch
- soutenu
- relevé
- sustained
- percussive

- pirouette
- spotting
- triplet
- swing
- fall
- recovery

LESSON 3

LESSON INTRODUCTION

When students enter the room, seat them in their warm-up spots facing the audience.

Go over the outcomes for the lessons.

➡ We have learned a warm-up and plyometrics. I should see a huge improvement today in your performance of both the warm-up and the plyometrics. After we do our warm-up and plyometrics, we'll do movement combinations that will improve

our skill-related fitness components. What are the skill-related fitness components? [Agility, balance, coordination, power, reaction time, speed.]

Let's do our warm-up. [Turn on music and say, "5, 6, 7, 8." Students will complete warm-up, and you will coach for improvement.]

We have finished our warm-up. Line up for plyometrics.

Remember to count and come in on time for each skill. I will call out each skill and start the first group with "5, 6, 7, 8." Remember that we start on the count of 1 with the right foot from the stage-left side of the space, and on the count of 1 with the left foot from the stage-right side of the space. Be ready! I'm going to turn on the music and start the first group. [Turn on music and count "5, 6, 7, 8." Call out each skill from the Plyometrics handout.]

Good job with plyometrics. Do a skip over to your warm-up spot and have a seat. [Students do this.] Now we will work on **reaction time**. When we do the next exercise, there will be no talking or laughing. When I blow my whistle (or other device), everyone will begin walking on the beat of the music. You may go anywhere in the room you like as long as you *fill up all of the space in the room and do not bump into anyone else.* When I blow my whistle the next time, freeze. I will call out another locomotor movement (such as run), and when I blow my whistle, everyone will start running on the beat of the music, again filling up all of the space in the room and not bumping into anyone else. We will do this for a variety of locomotor movements. The idea is for you to freeze as quickly as you can or to start as quickly as you can. You are reacting to the whistle. By practicing reacting, you improve your reaction time. This means you can more quickly react to the opponent you are guarding, or you can react more quickly to intercept a pass. What are some other examples of how having a quick reaction time would be an advantage? [Students respond: emergencies, avoiding a collision.] Okay, let's begin. [Start the music, call out, "Walk," and blow the whistle. Do this for walk, jog, run, gallop, skip, slide, and grapevine. Remind students to fill up empty space in the room in between each movement you call out and not to talk.]

Good—we will keep working on that! Do a gallop to come to your warm-up spots. [Students move to their spots.] We will work on balance next.

Balance is very important in sports. If you have good balance, you can stay on your feet when your opponent tries to push you down. We can recover from an off-balance position or prevent a fall more easily. Balance comes from proper body alignment, base of support, sight, and your inner ears. We'll now do an experiment with balance.

- Stand up and place your feet parallel and shoulder-width apart. This is called parallel second position. [Students do this.] Is it easy to balance standing in this position? [Yes.] Why? [Our base of support is wide.]

- Now put your feet together. [Students do this.] Is it harder to balance? [Some will say yes, some will say no.] Why might it be harder to balance in this position? [Our base of support is narrower.]

- Now stand on only one foot. [Students do this.] Did balance get harder this time? Why? [Some might not have held their alignment when they put their weight on one foot, and the base of support is much narrower.]

- Now put both feet together again. This time, close your eyes (don't cheat!) and try to balance. [Students do this.] What did you feel happening in your body this time? [Wobbling, muscles in the feet moving, swaying, disorientation.] Why? [Sight was taken away and the rest of the body had to compensate, so balance was harder.]

- Now open your eyes, keep both feet together, and rise up onto your toes. [Students do this.] What changes did you notice? [Harder to hold alignment, feet have to make adjustments, wobbling.] Go up on your toes again and close your eyes. [Students do this.] Could you hold your balance? [Many will not be able to do this!]

- Now pick up one foot. Get your balance on one foot and rise up onto your toes. [Students do this.] Now what changes do you notice? [Alignment is harder, axis must be vertical and held with muscles, base of support is very small.] Can you hold your balance? [Many will not be able to do this!]

- Now sit down. You'll get better at skill-related fitness components with practice. Think about the ballerina who has to balance on one pointe shoe and turn three times while balanced. This is a normal thing for a ballerina to do. It takes lots of practice balancing on the pointe shoe and then balancing while turning. What could you do to practice balance while you talk on the phone? [Stand on one foot, stand on toes, stand on one foot up on toes and try to hold as long as possible, close eyes.] What are some ways you could practice balancing while doing other things? [Stand to put on socks and shoes, stand on toes while doing things.]

Note: Some students will not be able to balance on one foot, much less on the toes or with eyes shut. Encourage them to keep practicing and, if time permits, try this short exercise in several lessons.

Coordination is next. **Coordination** allows you to do several things at a time, like cradling a lacrosse ball while watching your opponent and running a play. The better coordinated you are, the more easily you can do any of the things you want to do. Things like chores, taking a shower, playing with the dog, and playing an instrument require coordination. Just like balance, coordination is improved by practice. We will try some coordination patterns using isolations. **Isolations** involve moving only one part of the body at a time. They are often used in jazz dance. If you mess up, it's okay. You can start again. Remember, coordination takes practice! We'll try one body part, then try to add others. Let's see how we do!

Note: If students have trouble doing this on the fast beat, start out with a movement on every other count (1, 3, 5, 7 in a slow beat) until they get the hang of it.

Head

- First, you will just move your head: R, L, R, L, R, L, R, L, taking 8 counts. Do not snap your head; just put it in each new position. [Count while students do this.]

- Now the head goes down, up, down, up, down, up, down, up, taking 8 counts. [Count while students do this.]

- Now the head goes L, R, L, R, L, R, L, R, taking 8 counts. [Count while students do this.]
- Now the head goes up, down, up, down, up, down, up, down, taking 8 counts. [Count while students do this.]
- Now, I'm going to put on music and you will combine all four patterns. Be sure to count! [Put on music, count "5, 6, 7, 8" to start, and do the right-to-left portion, followed by the down-to-up portion, followed by left-to-right portion, followed by up-to-down portion. Practice this a few times.]
- Now let's try this on 4 counts instead of 8. Each part will get only 4 counts of music, then the next part starts. [Try it.]
- Now let's try this on 2 counts. [Try it.] You can see that it was harder to coordinate on 2 counts than it was on 8 counts.
- Now let's try this on 1 count. That means head moves R, L, down, up, L, R, up, down. [Try it.] Was that even harder?

Shoulders

- Now you will move your shoulders using the same pattern as your head. On the right-to-left part, only that shoulder will move. On the down-to-up part and on the up-to-down part, both shoulders will move together. [Start music, count "5, 6, 7, 8," and try it.]
- Now let's try this on 4 counts instead of 8. [Try it.]
- Now let's try this on 2 counts. [Try it.]
- Now let's try this on 1 count. That means the shoulders move R, L, down, up, L, R, up, down. [Try it.] Was that even harder?

Ribs

- The next combination is with the ribs. To move the ribs, you have to lift up your **diaphragm.** Put your hands on your ribs and lift up. Don't use your shoulders at all. Let's try lifting a couple times. [Do this.]
- The rib combination is R, L, R, L, R, L, R, L, then front, back, front, back, front, back, front, back, then L, R, L, R, L, R, L, R, then back, front, back, front, back, front, back, front. You will try this on 8 counts, 4 counts, 2 counts, and 1 count just like you've done the other coordination patterns. [Try these.]

Note: Some students might have trouble isolating their ribs. Assure them that the ribs are the most difficult, and that as they try more often, the ribs *will* move. Practice!

Hips

- Now you will isolate the hips. Only the hips can move! The pattern is this: R, L, R, L, R, L, R, L, then a big 8-count circle to the right; then L, R, L, R, L, R, L, R, then a big 8-count circle to the left. [Turn on music, count "5, 6, 7, 8," and students try this.]
- Now let's try this on 4 counts. [Try it.]
- Now let's try 2 counts. [Try it.]
- Now let's try this on 1 count. That means the hips move R, L, down, up, L, R, up, down. [Try it.] Was that even harder?

Isolation Challenge

- Now for a challenge. Let's do the head, shoulders, ribs, and hips right straight through without stopping (on DVD). We'll use the 8-count pattern for all of them. [Do it to music.]
- Let's try that on 4 counts! [Do it to music.]
- Okay, now for the real challenge: 2 counts, twice in a row, without stopping! [Try it to music.]
- Let's try it on 1 to see what happens. [Usually lots of laughs, but some students will want to perfect 1.]

Other Ideas for Variety and Challenge in Coordination

- Make up isolation combinations using one, two, or three body parts at a time.
- Add steps to the isolation combination, such as four steps forward and four steps backward, or step–step–step–touch.
- Try the patterns while walking across the floor (during plyometrics), such as walk with your head isolation combination as you go across the floor.
- Do the combination facing each wall without any stop in between walls.
- Try the combination on 6 counts. It'll be a challenge to count to 6 when the music phrases are 8!
- For quadriceps strength, do the isolations in plié in second position (wide feet, knees bent).
- The possibilities are endless. We'll have fun making up a coordination pattern and teaching it to the class!

Note: If time permits, do more isolations as part of other lessons.

LESSON 4

LESSON INTRODUCTION

When students enter the room, seat them in their warm-up spots facing the audience.

Go over the outcomes for the lessons.

We will begin with warm-up and plyometrics. [Students do this.]

Note: Depending on class length, students' ability, amount of correction needed, and students' desire to perfect combinations, lessons 3 and 4 can take more than one class each. You can decide where to break and how many class periods to use. It is important for students to experience all of the combinations.

Have a seat for a minute. Yesterday we had fun with coordination, and we can do some more of that again later if there's time. Remember, coordination takes practice. Now we are going to do some work with **changing weight.** Being able to change weight helps with agility and balance. How can you change weight? [From two feet to one foot, two feet to two feet, one foot to two feet, one foot to one foot.]

- Stand up and let's try some weight changes. Jump on two feet 8 times. [Count while students jump.]
- Now change from one foot to the other foot for 8 counts. [Count while students do this.]
- Next, try alternating two feet, one foot (R), two feet, one foot (L) for 8 counts. [Count while students do this.]

- Now we will try a combination of changing weight (on DVD).
  - Count 1: hop on R foot.
  - Count 2: jump on both feet shoulder-width apart.
  - Count 3: hop on L foot.
  - Count 4: jump on both feet shoulder-width apart.
  - Count 5: jump on both feet with R in front of L.
  - Count 6: jump on both feet with feet wide apart.
  - Count 7: jump on both feet with L in front of R.
  - Count 8: hop on R foot. We will do this very slowly while I count. [Do this.]
- Now we will reverse what we just did.
  - Count 1: hop on L foot.
  - Count 2: jump on both feet shoulder-width apart.
  - Count 3: hop on R foot.
  - Count 4: jump on both feet shoulder-width apart.
  - Count 5: jump on both feet with L in front of R.
  - Count 6: jump on both feet with feet wide apart.
  - Count 7: jump on both feet with R in front of L.
  - Count 8: hop on L foot. We will do this very slowly while I count. [Do this.]
- Now, let's do the weight-changing combination alternating sides: first R, then L. [Start music, cue "5, 6, 7, 8," and do combination.]
- What other fitness component was involved in the weight-changing combination? [Coordination, balance, cardiorespiratory endurance.]

Note: Have students make up weight-changing combinations. Encourage brain teasers, but make sure the student who creates the combination can demonstrate it to the class!

- Now we will do a different kind of weight change—one with traveling. In a minute, we will walk around just like we did for reaction time.
- When I blow the whistle, you try to hold your balance on the foot you last stepped on. Start walking again at the whistle. Try taking big steps and challenging yourself with balance. Okay, get up and let's see what happens as we try this. We will not be using music for this, only a whistle. Do not talk. Start walking at the speed of your choice. [Try it.]
- Let's do the same thing with fast walks this time. [Do it.]
- And now let's try this with runs. [Do it.]

Have a seat in your warm-up spot. [Students do this.] Now we are going to experiment with different types of turns. Sometimes people become disoriented and lose their balance when they turn. In sports, it is necessary to track your opponent at all times in order to have an effective defense. Often, the best way to stay with your opponent is to turn. Turning efficiently with balance and without becoming disoriented takes practice. We are going to try these turns one at a time. Be patient with yourself. Some people are natural turners and can do this easily. Other people need a lot of practice but it's still hard for them to turn. When you do your turns, I will count "5, 6, 7, 8" and everyone will turn in the same direction at the same time.

 All of the following movements are demonstrated on the DVD.

Jump Turn

➡ Now we'll work on a **jump turn**. Facing downstage with feet in parallel second position, bend both knees (**demi-plié**) to prepare to jump. Jump, lifting both feet off the floor at the same time and keeping the body aligned. Make a quarter turn to the right in the air, and land on both feet with both knees bent. You will be facing stage right. [Try it.] Now do another quarter turn to the right to face upstage. [Try it.] Now another quarter turn to face stage left. [Try it.] And one more to face the audience. [Try it.] Now let's do the same thing to the left. I'll count "5, 6, 7, 8" and you do 4 quarter turns left. [Try it.] Now let's do right and left without stopping: 5, 6, 7, 8. [Students do it.] Now let's do jump half turns right and left. We'll jump right on count 1 and hold for count 2, then jump right on count 3 and hold on count 4, then jump left on count 5 and hold on count 6, then jump left on count 7 and hold on count 8. Okay, 5, 6, 7, 8. [Students do it.] Now let's try jump full turns. We'll jump right on count 1 and hold counts 2, 3, 4; then jump left on count 5 and hold counts 6, 7, 8. Now 5, 6, 7, 8. [Students do this.] Now let's try putting quarter, half, and full turns together with music. Here we go: 5, 6, 7, 8. [Students do this. Try it in parallel first position—harder to balance!]

Three-Step Turn

➡ Now let's try the **three-step turn.** With feet in parallel first position, face downstage and step to the side with the right foot (step 1, count 1). Step your left foot across the right foot to face upstage (step 2, count 2). Continue the turn to the right by stepping with the right foot to face downstage (the starting position) (step 3, count 3). Hold on count 4. [Walk through it with students several times, counting slowly. Then walk through it on the left side several times. Then alternate right and left three-step turns. Then speed it up and do it to music.] Now we'll try some variations. First, end with a touch of the ball of the foot on count 4. A **touch** has no weight. [Demonstrate and try this.] Next, add a clap as you touch. [Try this.] Other variations to try: kick on count 4, snap on count 4, vary arm positions while turning and on count 4 (overhead, behind back, out to sides, and so on).

Paddle Turn

➡ Let's work on the **paddle turn.** Start with feet in parallel first position and weight on left foot with knee slightly bent. Then step downstage lightly with the ball of the right foot while turning to face stage left (count 1). Immediately transfer

weight back to the left foot and face upstage (count 2). Step upstage lightly with the ball of the right foot while turning to face stage right (count 3). Immediately transfer weight back to the left foot and face the audience (count 4). Try this with me several times. Each time you use the ball of the foot, it is a paddle. We could take four paddles to make a full turn instead of the two we just did. *Paddle* comes from using the foot like an oar to steer the turn. Let's do the paddle turn left. [Try it.] Now let's do some paddle turns to music. [Try it.] Other variations to try: use different arms, turn right, turn left, rise higher on each paddle, lower the body on each paddle, or hold between each paddle.]

Soutenu

The **soutenu** (pronounced soo-te-new) is a turn done this way: Stand with feet in second position parallel. Place right foot over the left foot. Rise up to the balls of both feet (**relevé**) and twist around to the left while letting the feet unwind, and finish facing the way you started. The left foot will be in front when you finish. [Try it crossing left foot over right and then try these variations: reverse feet, change body level, create new arm patterns, make a **sustained** (smooth) turn, or make a **percussive** (sharp) turn.]

Pirouette

For the **pirouette,** start with two feet on the floor and push off the right foot to lift the right foot to the left knee. Spin (rotate) on the ball of the left foot with a straight left leg either clockwise or counterclockwise with the lifted right foot securely positioned against the left (supporting) knee. When the rotation is completed, return the lifted right foot to the floor. [Try it on both legs, turning both right and left on each leg.] Something that helps when you turn is called **spotting.** Let's try something to learn how to spot. Do this with me. Look at the audience and slowly turn your body to the right. Just take little steps with your feet to turn, and keep looking at the audience as long as you can. When you have turned so far that you cannot keep looking at the audience, whip your head around to look at the audience as you complete the turn. If you spot, you will not get dizzy when you turn. Now spot with me turning left. We'll go slowly again. Now let's try some variations on the pirouette and try to spot. [Try these variations: change position of the lifted leg, change the position of the arms, end balanced on one foot, or try to spin more than once (double pirouette). Note: Always do turns both ways, not just to one side.]

Sometimes your footwork is even, and sometimes it needs to be uneven, or in a rhythm that feels different than the usual way of doing the footwork. **Triplets** are groups of three steps. Practicing triplets is a good way to improve footwork. All three steps should travel the same distance.

Triplet

Step downstage on the right foot (in demi-plié, which means bent knee). Step downstage on the left foot (in relevé, with a straight knee). Step downstage on the right foot (in relevé, with a straight knee). Be sure to step on the ball of the foot. Simplified: step down (demi-plié), step up (relevé), step up (relevé). Say to yourself, "Down, up, up," or "1, 2, 3." [Try it and then try these variations: go forward, go backward, travel in a circle, do two triplets forward and two back, add arms.]

Swinging movement is also a big part of sports. All of the turns, the triplets, and swinging movements help your agility. Can you give an example of a movement that reminds you of swinging? [A fence gate, a clock pendulum, a door opening.] We are going to practice movements that **swing.** You will feel the sensation of weightlessness at the top of the swinging movement.

Swing

 Place your feet in parallel second position. Move the whole body from side to side, imitating the path of a swing. The weight will transfer from one foot to the other, and you will notice that the level of the swing is higher on the sides than it is in the middle. You will feel an up-and-down motion, like a swing. [Try it.] Now swing just your arms. [Try side to side, forward and backward.] Now let's swing a leg. [Try side to side, forward and backward.] Move various body parts (arm, leg) from side to side or forward and backward. [Try these variations: change the speed, change body levels, walk forward or backward while swinging the body or body parts, travel in a circle while swinging the body or body parts.]

Everyone knows that when you play a sport, part of the game is falling down and getting up. This is called **fall and recover.** If an athlete can do this quickly, the opponent will not be able to get away. Good balance often keeps you from falling, but the ability to fall without getting hurt and to get up pays off.

Fall and Recover

 What are some reasons why things might fall? [Being pushed off something, a slow leak in a balloon, a parachute landing, having the wind knocked out of you, fainting, pretending that your body has no bones.] What do we have to do to fall without getting hurt? [Keep abs tight, bend as low as possible before hitting the floor, use body parts that are cushioned, fall in the direction of the momentum, fall with the intention of getting right up, fall and roll. Have students look at the DVD, then try it. Also try these variations: change the speed, change body levels, change the direction (forward, backward, sideways), walk forward or backward, or travel in a circle.]

CLOSURE

- Did we meet all of our outcomes for today? If not, why not?
- What was hard and what was easy? [Counting, balance, isolations, coordination, staying on the beat of the music, remembering the sequence of movement, fall and recovery.]
- What must you do to handle the difficult parts of this lesson? [Practice.]
- Name the skill-related components of physical fitness. [Students can look at their handouts.]
- I encourage you to practice these skills at home.
- In the next class, you will start to work on your sports dance.

NOTE FOR TEACHERS

It is likely that students will want to do more than just try all of the skills presented in this lesson. If time permits, spend time practicing each skill before moving on to the next skill.

EXTENSION

If time permits, let students experiment on their own or with a partner with each skill for a couple of minutes and watch for unique movement. Ask the students with unique movement to show the class. Try to select different students to show their movements.

5, 6, 7, & 8

SPORTS DANCE PROJECT

The project for this unit can be completed in four lessons (5, 6, 7, and 8), although you can add more lessons if you think it is necessary. Outcomes, National Dance Standards, and materials listed immediately after this apply to all of the project's lessons, whereas each lesson has its own distinct preparation.

OUTCOMES

- Students will create movement combinations for performance.
- Students will complete a Pathways Map.
- Students will complete a Daily Contribution Sheet.
- Students will perform for an audience.
- Students will write a critique using a criteria sheet.

NATIONAL DANCE STANDARDS

- Identifying and demonstrating movement elements and skills in performing dance
- Understanding choreographic principles, processes, and structures
- Understanding dance as a way to create and communicate meaning
- Applying and demonstrating critical-thinking and creative-thinking skills in dance
- Making connections between dance and healthful living
- Making connections between dance and other disciplines

MATERIALS

- Music player with enough volume for the class space
- Instrumental CDs previously used in class
- Music player for each group (students may bring these in if not available for the class)
- Pathways Map
- Pathways Map Instructions
- Daily Contribution Sheet for the number of days students will have to work on their projects (use the multiday sheet if more than three days of lessons)

• Sports Dance Criteria handout

• Choreographing a Dance handout

• Critique Guidelines handout

• Sports Dance Self-Assessment handout

• Sports Dance Group Assessment handout

• Teacher's Assessment of Performance

• Sports Dance Project Rubric

• Audience Etiquette sign

• Bring a Pencil sign

• Workstation signs

• Optional: Deal-a-Dance Cards included with *Building Dances* or *Building More Dances*; use these cards to assist students in their choreography, **if needed:**

  • Turns: green cards 5, 41, 51, 61, 74, 79, 83

  • Triplet: green card 7

  • Fall and recover: green cards 142, 153

  • Swing: green card 172

• Paper clips or folders

PREPARATION

• Before beginning today's lesson, read the extension at the end of lesson 8.

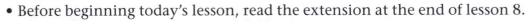
• Give a copy of the Critique Guidelines to the language arts department and ask them to go over the material if not already done. (Do this before lesson 1 if possible.)

• Run off Pathways Map, Pathways Map Instructions, Daily Contribution Sheet, Sports Dance Criteria handout, and Choreographing a Dance handout for every student. Note: Copy Pathways Map and Pathways Map Instructions on opposite sides of one sheet of paper.

• On the wall, post workstation numbers for the number of groups in the class, or use cones, or put tape on the floor.

• Laminate Deal-a-Dance Cards, if you are using them.

• Laminate and post Bring a Pencil and Audience Etiquette signs on the walls of the teaching area.

• Post outcomes for this lesson.

• Post vocabulary for this lesson.

• Devise a way to select the groups for the projects. For example, students can draw numbers or colors, students can select, you can select, or you can play selections of performance music and allow students to form groups according to the music they like.

• Select tracks of music for the projects (twice as many tracks as the number of performance groups in the class so there are plenty of choices).

SPORTS DANCE CRITERIA

- Work in groups of 4 or 5 students.
- Dance must be 2 to 3 minutes long.
- Use the choreographic process (Choreographing a Dance h...
- Use all of the space in the performance area.
- Use at least 4 different locomotor (traveling) movements.
- Use at least 4 different levels (high, medium, low, floor).

AUDIENCE ETIQUETTE

Be Attentive
- Watch the dance carefully.
- Do not talk.

Supportive
- Act interested.
- Respect the effort of the performers.

CHOREOGRAPHING A DANCE

1. Choose the motivation: *theme, story line, movement phrase.*
2. Create movements using the elements of choreography:
   - Different **rhythms** (timing):

PATHWAYS MAP

Name

Audience

DAILY CONTRIBUTION SHEET
(TWO-DAY)

Name_____ Class_____

Day 1 contributions

PATHWAYS MAP INSTRUCTIONS

Name_____ Class_____

CRITIQUE GUIDELINES

Critique—A critique is an analysis of what one sees in a performance based on the criteria for the performance. It is not a criticism, although it may state that some of the criteria were not met and why.
Each student will write a critique of two of the group performances. The critique will be of the whole group, not of any individual in the group. The critique will meet these guidelines:

- The critique will be written or typed in good form.
- Use 12-point font for typed work.
- The critique will be hand written or printed in black ink ONLY.
- Handwriting must be neat and legible.
- The critique will contain paragra...
- complete sentence...

WORKSTATION 1

BRING A PENCIL TO CLASS

VOCABULARY

- Daily Contribution Sheet
- Pathways Map
- syncopated
- scattered
- zigzag
- twisted
- angular
- symmetrical
- asymmetrical
- AB
- ABA
- call and response
- canon
- reordering
- retrograde

UNIT II
DANCE FOR ATHLETES

LESSON 5

LESSON INTRODUCTION

When students enter the room, seat them in their warm-up spots facing the audience.

Go over the outcomes for the lesson.

 We'll begin class today with our warm-up. [Turn music on and count "5, 6, 7, 8." Students do warm-up.]

Today we are going to begin our sports dance project. You will work in groups of four or five people. Each of you will complete your Pathways Map and a Daily Contribution Sheet showing what you did in each lesson. Each group will perform their project for the class. After the performances, you will complete a self-assessment of your project and a group assessment of one of the groups in the class. And after the performances, you will write a critique from a criteria sheet. You will practice and perform your sports dance to music. I have selected a lot of possibilities for performance music. It all has a good beat. Your group will be able to select their music, but no two groups may use the same music.

As I just said, each person will complete a Pathways Map and a Daily Contribution Sheet. I will hand out these sheets and we will go over them. Neatly write your name on each sheet, but do not write anything else on the sheets until I give the instructions. [Pass out Pathways Maps, Pathways Map Instructions, Daily Contribution Sheets, and pencils if needed.]

Let's look at the **Daily Contribution Sheet** first. In each lesson, while you are working on your projects, you will need to write what you have contributed to the group on your Daily Contribution Sheet. Completing the Daily Contribution Sheet thoroughly and accurately is part of your grade for the project, so you want to be sure to do a good job. (An example of a contribution is "I made up the arm movement for our runs.")

Now let's look at the *instructions* for the **Pathways Map**. This sheet is an example of how someone might do the map. This example is *not* for anyone to copy. Look in the lower-right corner of the paper and find the word *Start*. When you start working in your group, you will write *Start* on your map in the place on the floor where you, personally, start to move. The arrows show the path and direction you move. Look at the box with 2 in it. You will see that the student in the example drew an arrow from 1, *Start*, to 3, and wrote along the arrow line 2 what movement that person did. Look at 3. In the example, the student wrote the movement that she did in that location. From 3, she took a crazy path to 5; along the arrow line 4 she wrote the movement she did while traveling along this path. Does everyone understand how to complete a Pathways Map? [Answer any questions.] Keep your Pathways Map with you, and as your group plans their movement for the project, write your paths and movements on your Pathways Map. Be sure to use pencil because as your group works, your movement and pathways might change and you will need to erase and correct your map.

I am passing out Choreographing a Dance and Sports Dance Criteria. [Pass these out.] Neatly write your name on each sheet. [Students do this.] Let's look at **Choreographing a Dance** first. This explains the process of creating or making up a dance. Your group will follow the process on the sheet. It's a good idea to write your ideas on these sheets so you won't forget what you created from lesson to lesson.

You might need to explain some of the terms on the Choreographing a Dance handout:

- **Syncopated** is an uneven rhythm, like kick–ball–change (count of "1 *and* 2" rather than even counts).
- **Scattered** means irregular random formation or with no identifiable shape.
- **Zigzag** is a series of diagonals.
- **Twisted** looks like a corkscrew.
- **Angular** means sharp angles of body parts.
- **Symmetrical** is even on both sides (for example, both arms held at the same height or the same number of dancers on both sides of the space).
- **Asymmetrical** is uneven or unbalanced from side to side.
- **AB** is a two-part composition with two distinct self-contained sections; one is called A and the other is called B. The two parts share something, like style, tempo, or movement quality.
- **ABA** is a composition with A and B performed as normal. The second time A is performed, it is changed in some way, such as shorter or longer or abbreviated.
- **Call and response** occurs when a soloist or group performs, then the second soloist or group performs in response to the first.
- **Canon** involves groups performing the same movement beginning at different times. "Row, Row, Row Your Boat" is a canon.
- **Reordering** is changing the order of the counts of a movement.
- **Retrograde** is doing a movement backward (reversing the counts).

Now let's look at the **Sports Dance Criteria** handout. This lists the minimum that each group must have in the dance in order to get the maximum points. Your group is free to add as much as you want—your dance is your creation! Read the handouts as a group before you begin working on your sports dance. Work as a group to decide how you all will meet the criteria listed on the handout. Make sure the movement you select is appropriate and safe.

At the end of each class, you will turn in all of your handouts: Pathways Map, Daily Contribution Sheet, Choreographing a Dance, and Sports Dance Criteria. We'll put them in folders so they'll be ready for your group at the next class. Do you have any questions before you get into your groups and begin working? [Either allow students to choose their own groups, or assign groups based on sports interest or any other method.] Once you have your group together, we'll listen to the music selections, and your group can tell me which selection you will use. As soon as we

select music, groups can come up and I will assign your group a workstation. The workstation numbers are on the walls. Begin work as soon as you arrive at your station. [Allow students to work in the time remaining. Circulate to monitor and answer questions. Do not tell students how to do the project; they have to figure that out for themselves. Remind each group to complete their Daily Contribution Sheet and Pathways Map as they work.]

CLOSURE

➡ Do a gallop to come over and have a seat. Bring your Pathways Maps, Daily Contribution Sheets, Choreographing a Dance, Sports Dance Criteria, and pencils with you. [Students come over.] We made a lot of progress today. Today was the hardest part: getting all the instructions and getting started. Tomorrow and the next lesson after we warm up, you will have almost the entire class to work on your project. You will perform your project for the class in the following lesson (or whatever lesson that's been decided). Tomorrow we will also go over the Sports Dance Project Rubric at the beginning of class. Put your Pathways Map and Daily Contribution Sheets together. One person in each group will collect them and bring them to me. [Have paper clips to clip together the sheets for each group and use a folder for each group. This will save time when handing them out on subsequent lessons.]

- Did we meet our outcomes for today?
- Are there any problems we need to resolve?
- Are there any questions?

═══ LESSON 6 ═══

PREPARATION

- Have selected music ready.
- Have folders for Pathways Map, Daily Contribution Sheets, Choreographing a Dance, Sports Dance Criteria in the class space.
- Run off enough copies of Sports Dance Project Rubric for all students.
- Have pencils available.
- Post vocabulary and outcomes for the lesson, stage direction signs, Audience Etiquette sign, and Bring a Pencil sign (if not still posted from lesson 5).

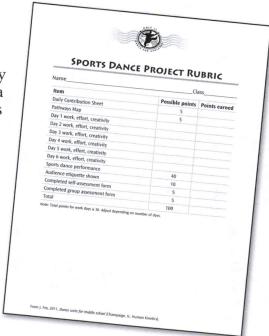

LESSON INTRODUCTION

When students enter the room, seat them in their warm-up spots facing the audience.

Go over the outcomes for the lesson.

 Let's warm up. [Play music.] 5, 6, 7, 8. [Students warm up.]

Before we begin working on our projects, we'll look at the Sports Dance Project Rubric. [Pass out Sports Dance Project Rubric sheets and pencils, if needed.] As soon as you get your sheet, neatly write your name and class period on it. [Students do this.] On performance day, each of you will be scored using this rubric. Notice that how you work in each lesson is part of the scoring. Completing your Pathways Map and Daily Contribution Sheet is also part of your score. When you worked yesterday, you saw that there were criteria, which means required movements, on your Sports Dance Criteria sheets. Points are awarded for including all of the criteria in your project. Performance requirements means that your group obviously practiced your project and performed it seriously, with strong movement, and with a very good attitude. You'll notice that you are also scored on your audience etiquette. That means demonstrating the behaviors listed on the Audience Etiquette signs that have been posted in the class since we started our unit on dance for athletes. At the bottom of the Sports Dance Project Rubric, notice that points are awarded for completing your self-assessment and group assessment, which we will talk about tomorrow. Does anyone have any questions about the scoring for the project?

Everyone hand in your Sports Dance Project Rubric; pick up your Pathways Map, Daily Contribution Sheet, Choreographing a Dance, and Sports Dance Criteria; and go to your stations to begin your work. I will play the music the groups have chosen several times during class.

As you play the music and circulate, notice the students' progress. Remind them that they must work efficiently because they have only one more (or however many more lessons time permits) lesson to work. Some groups will get to work and organize their project quickly. Encourage them to practice many times for perfection. Other groups may need motivation. Encourage cooperation, courtesy, compromise, and selecting a captain if leadership is lacking. Also mention that home practice is needed so that everyone in the group can do the movements well.

CLOSURE

Do a grapevine to come over. Hand in your Daily Contribution Sheet, Pathways Maps, Choreographing a Dance, Sports Dance Criteria, and borrowed pencils. Have a seat. [Collect sheets and pencils.] Remember to practice at home. Tomorrow is the last lesson to work on the project in class. If your group needs ideas, talk with parents and friends and bring ideas back to class.

- Did we meet our outcomes for today?

- Are there any problems we need to resolve?

- Are there any questions?

LESSON 7

PREPARATION

- Have music ready.
- Have folders with Pathways Maps, Daily Contribution Sheets, Choreographing a Dance, Sports Dance Criteria, and Sports Dance Project Rubric in the class space.
- Have pencils in the class space.
- Mark off the performance space with cones, tape, or flags: 36 feet wide by 30 feet deep (11 by 9 m).

- Post vocabulary and outcomes for the lesson, stage direction signs, Audience Etiquette sign, and Bring a Pencil sign (if not still posted from lesson 5).

LESSON INTRODUCTION

When students enter the room, seat them in their warm-up spots facing the audience. Go over the outcomes for the lesson.

➡ Let's warm up first. [Start music.] 5, 6, 7, 8. [Students do the warm-up.]

Today is the last lesson (or next-to-last lesson or whatever has been decided) to work in your groups. At our next class, each group will perform the sports dance. As you work today, your group will practice in the performance space when your music is played. Take a look at the performance space that is marked off with cones (tape, flags). I'll call out which group is next, and that group needs to quickly move to the performance space for their turn. One person from each group will pick up the Pathways Maps, Daily Contribution Sheets, Choreographing a Dance, Sports Dance Criteria, and pencils. Go to your stations and complete your project. [As students work, circulate, alternate playing music for each group, and note progress. If you think that an additional lesson of work would yield better results, or if students are working hard and are not finished, consider adding an extra lesson of group work.]

CLOSURE

➡ Jog to come over and have a seat. One person from each group collect the Pathways Maps, Daily Contribution Sheets, Choreographing a Dance, Sports Dance Criteria, and pencils and turn them in.

- **Option 1.** You have worked very hard for the past three lessons. The projects are complete. Tomorrow we will watch each group perform their sports dance. I am excited to see what the groups have done. I saw some very creative and fun projects. [In this case, move on to lesson 8 in the next class.]

- **Option 2.** Each group has been working very hard, and it looks like everyone's project would benefit from having one more lesson (or whatever seems necessary) to work and practice. Make sure you practice at home as well. [In this case, repeat lesson 7 as many times as necessary before moving on to lesson 8.]

• Did we meet our outcomes for today?
• Are there any problems we need to resolve?
• Are there any questions?

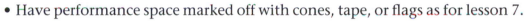

LESSON 8

PREPARATION

 • Have rubrics for each group clipped together.

 • Have folders for Pathways Maps, Daily Contribution Sheets, Choreographing a Dance, and Sports Dance Criteria in the class space.

 • Put due date on the Critique Guidelines handout.

 • Run off enough copies of the Teacher's Assessment of Performance for each group.

 • Run off enough copies of Sports Dance Group Assessment, Sports Dance Self-Assessment, and Critique Guidelines for all students.

• Have music ready.

• Have performance space marked off with cones, tape, or flags as for lesson 7.

• Post vocabulary and outcomes for the lesson, stage direction signs, Audience Etiquette sign, and Bring a Pencil sign (if not still posted from lesson 5).

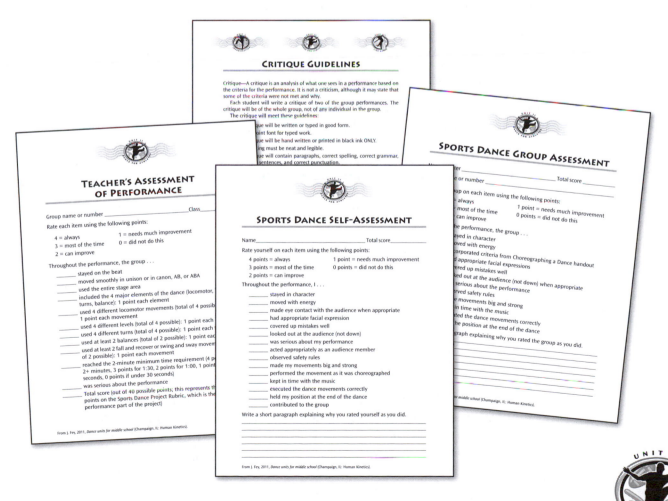

LESSON INTRODUCTION

When students enter the room, seat them in warm-up spots facing the audience. Go over the outcomes for the lesson.

➡️ We always warm up first. [Start music.] 5, 6, 7, 8. [Students warm up.]

We're all excited about performing our sports dances and about watching what other groups have done. You are going to have a short amount of time to run through your project *once* in the performance space with the music, then the groups will perform. Go to your stations and practice for your run-through in the performance space until it is your group's turn. [Allow about 15 minutes for this.]

Skip to come to the audience area, turn in your Pathways Map and Daily Contribution Sheet, and have a seat. Choreographing a Dance and Sports Dance Criteria are yours to keep. You will find them useful when you write your critique. [The wall that you have been using as audience, or downstage, is the audience area where students sit with their backs to the wall, facing the "stage" to watch the performances.] Which group would like to go first? [In some classes, everyone will volunteer. In other classes, no one will volunteer. Have a designated order, draw numbers, or use some other method to determine performance order.] What is the proper etiquette for the audience? [Students respond with what has been posted on the Audience Etiquette sign.] Give group _____ your attention. [Start the music. You may want to count "5, 6, 7, 8" to help each group begin. Use the Teacher's Assessment of Performance form while each group performs.]

At the end of each performance, insist that everyone applaud. Review audience etiquette, if necessary. Ask questions about each performance, such as these:

➡️
- What did you notice that was unusual?
- What movement caught your eye?
- What was interesting about this group's performance?
- Did the group meet the requirements of the project? How do you know this?
- Could you tell what sports this group was interested in from their movement?

Any other questions are fine, as long as they do not single out a particular student's performance.

CLOSURE

➡️ You all did very interesting sports dances and created movements that were fun to watch.

- What was most difficult about doing this project?
- What did you enjoy most about the project?
- To finish our unit, you will fill out a Sports Dance Self-Assessment and a Sports Dance Group Assessment for your performance. You will also write a sports dance critique of two of the groups. The assessments and critique are homework. The assessments are due the next class, and the critique is due

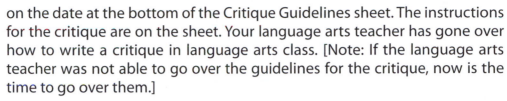

on the date at the bottom of the Critique Guidelines sheet. The instructions for the critique are on the sheet. Your language arts teacher has gone over how to write a critique in language arts class. [Note: If the language arts teacher was not able to go over the guidelines for the critique, now is the time to go over them.]

• Be sure to meet the deadlines for each of these three assignments. Pick up these three sheets on your way out.

NOTE FOR TEACHERS

 Complete the Sports Dance Project Rubric for each student. The lesson 5, lesson 6, and lesson 7 work, effort, and creativity can be completed after the last working lesson. If you decide to have the students work four lessons, combine the lesson 7 and lesson 8 work, effort, and creativity.

EXTENSION

• Some classes would enjoy performing their projects again. It might be possible to invite parents and other teachers and staff for a performance lesson. You can ask students on the second lesson of working on their projects if they would like to do this. Students can make invitations and deliver them to parents, their other teachers, the principal, and other staff in the school. You could also have invitations made up, and students could write in the lesson and time of the performance before they deliver them. If people who would not be comfortable sitting on the floor will attend, plan to have chairs available. See the section titled You Made It . . . Now What? (page 154) for other ideas.

• If time is available for another lesson, videotape the performances and have students watch the videos before writing their critiques. This gives them an opportunity to watch themselves performing.

UNIT THREE

JAZZ DANCE

1

INTRODUCTION AND WARM-UP

OUTCOMES

- Students will identify reasons why people dance.
- Students will learn correct technique for a variety of warm-up exercises.
- Students will practice executing warm-up exercises correctly to music.

NATIONAL DANCE STANDARDS

- Identifying and demonstrating movement elements and skills in performing dance
- Applying and demonstrating critical-thinking and creative-thinking skills in dance
- Demonstrating and understanding dance in various cultures and historical periods
- Making connections between dance and healthful living
- Making connections between dance and other disciplines

MATERIALS

- Music player with enough volume for the teaching space

- Music with a steady beat and appropriate lyrics (accompanying CD or see suggestions on page xxiii)

- Stage direction signs

- Audience Etiquette sign
- Handouts: Jazz Dance Warm-Up Chart, Rules for Safe Stretching, Foot and Arm Positions, Jazz Dance Collage and Homework Essay, Jazz Dance Collage and Homework Essay Rubric
- Projector (overhead or LCD) and laptop or dry-erase board
- Notebooks or folders for each student and a box to hold them

PREPARATION

This will take some time, but the materials are used through the unit.

 • Post outcomes for the lesson.

 • Post vocabulary for the lesson.

 • Laminate signs for Stage Right, Stage Left, Upstage, Downstage, Audience, and Audience Etiquette.

 • Put signs up on walls in teaching space following the Stage Directions Diagram (page 93).

• Make large versions of handouts or project them on a wall.

 • Write due dates and desired collage size on Jazz Dance Collage and Homework Essay sheet before running off handouts.

• Run off enough handouts for each student: Jazz Dance Warm-Up Chart (2-sided), Rules for Safe Stretching, Foot and Arm Positions, Jazz Dance Collage and Homework Essay, Jazz Dance Collage and Homework Essay Rubric.

• Post a list of the music that will be used.

• Ask the language arts teachers to go over the Critique Guidelines in language arts class.

VOCABULARY

• locomotor movement
• nonlocomotor (axial) movement
• warm-up
• across the floor
• center
• combination
• roll down and up

• head circle
• isolations
• reaches
• butterfly
• pike
• straddle
• lunge

LESSON INTRODUCTION

When students enter the room, seat them in their lines (squads) facing the wall chosen as the audience. Make sure lines are spread out so students can lie down without touching each other. Consider putting warm-up marks on the floor with tape if your students are not good at staying in their spaces:

Audience

X X X X X

X X X X X

X X X X X

X X X X X

X X X X X

Review outcomes for the lesson.

AUDIENCE ETIQUETT[E]

Be Attentive
- Watch the dance carefully.
- Do not talk.

Be Supportive
- Act interested.
- Respect the effort of the performers.

JAZZ DANCE WARM-UP CHART

Feet in parallel second position, turn on music, count "5, 6, 7, 8" to start.

Exercise	Counts	Body parts	Component
Roll down and up (2 times)	4 slow counts (16 counts total)	Spine	Flexibility, injury prevention
Head circles R and L	8 slow counts each (16 counts total)	Neck	Flexibility, coordination
Head isolations R to L (4 times)	8 slow counts	Neck	Flexibility, coordination
Head isolations up to down (4 times)	8 slow counts	Neck	Flexibility, coordination
Head isolations L to R (4 times)	8 slow counts	Neck	Flexibility, coordination
Head isolations down to up (4 times)	8 slow counts	Neck	Flexibility, coordination
Head isolations tilt R and L	8 slow counts	Neck	Flexibility, coordination

JAZZ DANCE COLLAGE AND HOMEWORK ESSAY

WHY PEOPLE DANCE

[...]AGE

[...] dance collage showing people dancing in a variety of circumstances. [...] various media (such as magazines, clip art, photos, Internet), gather [...] of people from various cultures dancing. All pictures should be attached

JAZZ DANCE COLLAGE AND HOMEWORK ESSAY RUBRIC

Name_____ Class_____

Item	Possible points	Points earned
Collage: neat, correct size	40	
Collage: variety of pictures	10	
Essay: introduction	5	
Essay: Why People Dance	20	
Essay: correct spelling	5	
Essay: correct grammar	5	
Essay: correct punctuation	5	
Essay: neat, legible, black ink	10	
Total	100	

From J. Fey, 2011, *Dance units for middle school* (Champaign, IL: Human Kinetics).

FOOT AND ARM POSITIONS

FOOT POSITIONS

Turned Out   Parallel

First position

Second position

Fourth position

RULES FOR SAFE STRETCHING

[...]tch *after* warming up.
[...]ys use proper technique for each stretch.
[...]ot bounce.
[...] stretch for 30 seconds.
[...] while stretching.
[...]ravity to your advantage.
[...]h in one plane.

CRITIQUE GUIDELINES

Critique—A critique is an analysis of what one sees in a performance based on the criteria for the performance. It is not a criticism, although it may state that some of the criteria were not met and why.

Each student will write a critique of two of the group performances. The critique will be of the whole group, not of any individual in the group. The critique will meet these guidelines:

[...]tten or typed in good form.
[...]yped work.
[...]en or printed in black ink ONLY.
[...]l legible.
[...]graphs, correct spelling, correct grammar,
[...]uation.
[...]date, and class in the upper-right
[...]Critique." The title
[...] of the first page.
[...]uction.
[...]s about each of the groups being
[...]uss the requirements for the dance, and suggestions
[...]alities of the group, and suggestions
[...]at you saw that proves why what you
[...]Be sure to identify the groups about
[...]ary.
[...] the day it is due.

[...]aign, IL: Human Kinetics).

JAZZ DANCE COLLA[GE] AND HOMEWORK ESSAY

Name_____

Item	Possible point[s]	
Collage: neat, correct size	40	
Collage: variety of pictures	10	
Essay: introduction	5	
Essay: Why People Dance	20	
Essay: correct spelling	5	
Essay: correct grammar	5	
Essay: correct punctuation	5	
Essay: neat, legible, black ink	10	
Total	100	

From J. Fey, 2011, *Dance units for middle school* (Champaign, IL: Human Kinetics).

• • • • • • • • • • • • AUDIENCE

From J. Fey, 2011, *Dance units for middle school* (Champaign, IL: Human Kinetics).

➡ We are beginning our unit on jazz dance. In this unit, you will determine why people dance, learn a jazz warm-up, learn locomotor (traveling) and nonlocomotor (axial) movements, and learn some basic jazz dance steps for a combination. In addition, you will choreograph a jazz dance, assess your own performance, assess the performance of a group, and write a critique.

We will begin our first lesson by determining why people dance. Why do people dance? [Make a list of students' responses on the board or project on the wall.] Here are some possible responses:

UNIT III
JAZZ DANCE

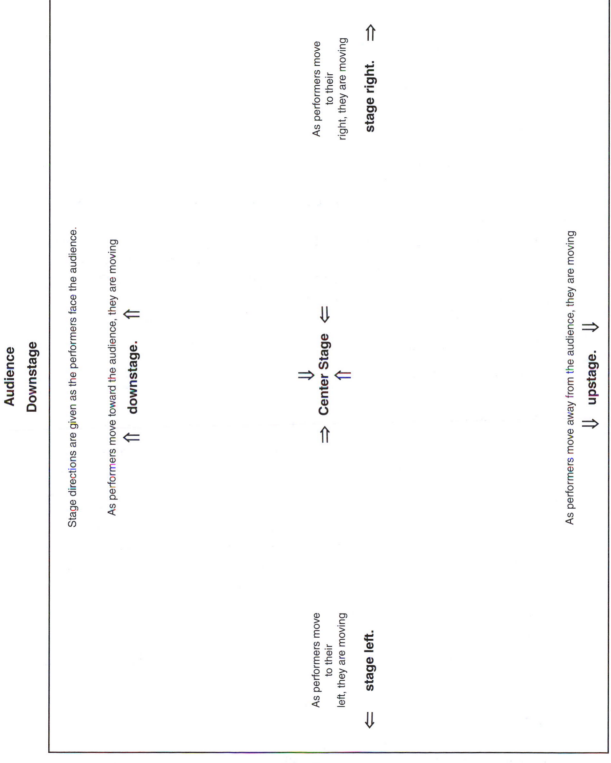

Stage Directions Diagram.

- Fun
- Means of communication
- Asking for rain or good crops
- Holidays and family milestones
- Treatment for physically and emotionally challenged people
- Social events

- Entertainment for an audience
- Worship
- Preparing for a hunt
- Weddings
- Exercise
- Physical therapy
- Cultural tradition

If you think about cultures all over the world, would you add any reasons to our list? [Add any new responses to the list.]

Do you know any dances from other countries or cultures? [Possible responses are hora—Israel, miserlou—Greece, troika—Russia, Virginia reel—USA, flamenco—Spain, jig—Ireland.]

Pay close attention to the music that we'll use during this unit. You will select one of the songs used in class for your jazz dance choreography. I will post a list of music we use each lesson. Be able to identify the music you would like to use for your choreography by lesson 4 of our unit.

Once we learn the skills, each lesson will be divided into four parts:

- **Warm-up:** to prepare the body for movement
- **Across the floor:** to learn locomotor movements (traveling dance steps)
- **Center:** to learn nonlocomotor (axial) movements (stationary dance steps)
- **Combination:** to put locomotor and nonlocomotor dance steps together

Today we will learn our jazz dance warm-up. Before we begin our warm-up, we need to take a look at three handouts. Neatly write your name and class on each handout when you receive it. The first is the Jazz Dance Warm-Up Chart. [Hand out Jazz Dance Warm-Up Chart.] This sheet lists all of the parts of the warm-up, the counts for each part, the body parts used, and the fitness component addressed. Keep this sheet next to you as we learn our warm-up. The second handout is Rules for Safe Stretching. [Hand out Rules for Safe Stretching.] Part of our warm-up is stretching. To prevent injury and improve flexibility, we need to stretch properly. Let's go over this handout now. [Go over handout.] Think about these rules when we stretch. Our feet need to be in parallel positions during our warm-up. [Hand out Foot and Arm Positions (page 95).] Let's stand up and practice our foot and arm positions before we begin our warm-up. [Do this.]

WARM-UP

Teach students the warm-up using the following coaching cues and the DVD if needed. Counts are listed with each exercise and on the Jazz Dance Warm-Up Chart. All counts are to the slow beat of the music. Demonstrate correct technique one exercise at a time or use the DVD. Students do the exercise while you watch and you count immediately after the demonstration. Correct students' technique immediately and have them repeat the performance, if necessary. Have poster-size

FOOT AND ARM POSITIONS

FOOT POSITIONS

Turned Out   Parallel

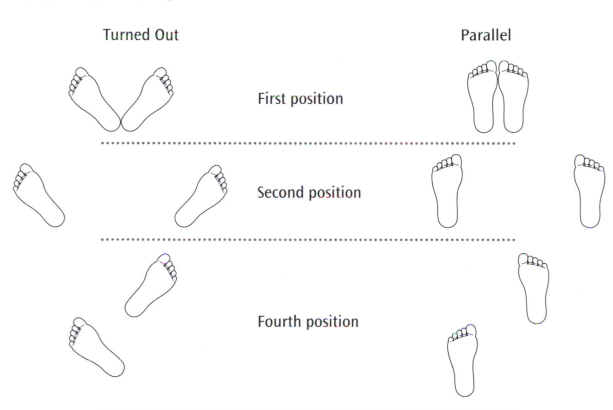

First position

Second position

Fourth position

ARM POSITIONS

First Position

Arms rounded, little fingers in front of thighs but not touching thighs, shoulders relaxed.

Second Position

Arms rounded, little fingers closest to the floor, hands in front of shoulders.

From J. Fey, 2011, *Dance units for middle school* (Champaign, IL: Human Kinetics).

warm-up charts posted on the audience wall in several spots or project them on a wall where all students can see them. Handouts go into the students' notebooks or folders.

Roll Down and Up
4 slow counts down, 4 slow counts up, done twice, total of 16 slow counts

- Feet are parallel and shoulder-width apart (second position parallel).
- Weight is on both feet and mostly on the balls of the feet the entire time.
- Top of head leads the way down, then neck, then upper back, then lower back.
- Arms, shoulders, and neck are relaxed the entire time.
- No pushing or straining; gravity does the work.
- Butt leads the way up, then lower back, then upper back, then neck, then head.
- Abdominal muscles pull you up.
- Use smooth and continuous movement down and up.
- Now we will roll down and up as listed on the warm-up chart. Count silently to yourself as I count. [Do this slowly with students a couple times and give corrections.]

Head Circles Right and Left
8 slow counts for each head circle, total of 16 slow counts

- Feet are parallel and shoulder-width apart (second position parallel).
- Totally relax the shoulders, neck, and arms.
- Abdominals are tight the entire time.
- Do not crank the head back; simply look up to the ceiling.
- Start by looking to the right, then chin to chest, then look left, then look up at ceiling, then look right, then chin to chest, and finish looking left. This is a head circle to the right.
- Reverse by starting to look to the left and end looking right.
- Now we will do head circles right and left as listed on the warm-up chart. Count silently to yourself as I count. [Do this slowly with students a couple times and give corrections. Do 8 slow counts for each head circle, for a total of 16 counts.]

Head Isolations Right to Left
4 times each side, total of 8 slow counts

- Feet are parallel and shoulder-width apart (second position parallel).
- Movement should be smooth—do not whip or snap the head.
- Totally relax the shoulders, neck, and arms.
- Abdominals are tight the entire time.
- Now we will do head isolations right and left as listed on the warm-up chart. Count silently to yourself as I count. [Do this slowly with students a couple times and give corrections. Look right and left 4 times each side for a total of 8 slow counts.]

Head Isolations Up to Down
4 times each, total of 8 slow counts

- Feet are parallel and shoulder-width apart (second position parallel).
- Movement should be smooth—do not whip or snap the head.
- Look up to the ceiling for *up*. Cranking the head back compresses vertebrae.
- Totally relax the shoulders, neck, and arms.
- Abdominals are tight the entire time.
- Now we will do head isolations up and down as listed on the warm-up chart. Count silently to yourself as I count. [Do this slowly with students a couple times and give corrections. Look up and down 4 times each for a total of 8 slow counts.]

Head Isolations Left to Right
4 times each, total of 8 slow counts

- Feet are parallel and shoulder-width apart (second position parallel).
- Movement should be smooth—do not whip or snap the head.
- Totally relax the shoulders, neck, and arms.
- Abdominals are tight the entire time.
- Now we will do head isolations left and right as listed on the warm-up chart. Count silently to yourself as I count. [Do this slowly with students a couple times and give corrections. Look left and right 4 times each for a total of 8 slow counts.]

Head Isolations Down to Up
4 times each, total of 8 slow counts

- Feet are parallel and shoulder-width apart (second position parallel).
- Movement should be smooth—do not whip or snap the head.
- Look up to the ceiling for *up*. Cranking the head back compresses vertebrae.
- Totally relax the shoulders, neck, and arms.
- Abdominals are tight the entire time.
- Now we will do all the exercises we've done so far on the warm-up chart. Count silently to yourself as I count. [Do this slowly with students a couple times and give corrections. Do roll down and up 2 times, head circles right and left for 8 slow counts, head isolations right and left 4 times, head isolations up and down 4 times, head isolations left and right 4 times, and head isolations down and up 4 times.]

Head Isolations Tilt Right and Left
Right and left 4 times each, total of 8 slow counts

- Feet are parallel and shoulder-width apart (second position parallel).
- Movement should be smooth—do not whip or snap the head.

- Ear should be over the shoulder on the tilt.
- Totally relax the shoulders, neck, and arms.
- Abdominals are tight the entire time.
- Now we will do head isolations tilt right and left as listed on the warm-up chart. Count silently to yourself as I count. [Do this slowly with students a couple times and give corrections. Tilt right and left 4 times each for a total of 8 slow counts.]

Shoulder Isolations Up to Down

Shoulders alternate moving up and down 4 times each, total of 8 slow counts

Note: The muscles in the neck and shoulders might tighten as students go through this isolation series. Have them gently tilt the head right and left until muscles relax. Tell students that as their muscles get used to isolations, the tightness will diminish.

- Feet are parallel and shoulder-width apart (second position parallel).
- Totally relax the neck and arms.
- Abdominals are tight the entire time.
- Do not hunch shoulders forward.
- Do not allow head to move forward.
- Keep head between shoulders the entire time.
- Lift shoulders to ears, then press shoulders down as low as possible.
- Now we will do shoulder isolations up and down as listed on the warm-up chart. Count silently to yourself as I count. [Do this slowly with students a couple times and give corrections. Alternate moving each shoulder up and down 4 times each for a total of 8 slow counts.]

Shoulder Isolations Back to Front

Shoulders alternate moving back and front 4 times each, total of 8 slow counts

- Feet are parallel and shoulder-width apart (second position parallel).
- Totally relax the neck and arms.
- Abdominals are tight the entire time.
- Do not hunch shoulders forward or arch the back.
- Do not allow head to move forward.
- Keep head between shoulders the entire time.
- Press shoulders as far back and forward as possible.
- Now we will do shoulder isolations back and front as listed on the warm-up chart. Count silently to yourself as I count. [Do this slowly with students a couple times and give corrections. Alternate moving each shoulder back and forth 4 times each for a total of 8 slow counts.]

Shoulder Isolations Backward Rolls
4 shoulder rolls backward, 2 counts for each roll, total of 8 slow counts

- Feet are parallel and shoulder-width apart (second position parallel).
- Totally relax the neck and arms.
- Abdominals are tight the entire time.
- Do not arch the back.
- Keep head between shoulders the entire time.
- Do not allow the head to move forward.
- Start by shrugging shoulders up, then roll them back, then down, and then forward. This is one complete roll backward and takes 2 counts.
- Now we will do shoulder isolations backward rolls as listed on the warm-up chart. Count silently to yourself as I count. [Do this slowly with students a couple times and give corrections. Do 4 shoulder rolls backward in 2 slow counts each for a total of 8 slow counts.]

Shoulder Isolations Forward Rolls
4 shoulder rolls forward, 2 counts for each roll, total of 8 slow counts

- Feet are parallel and shoulder-width apart (second position parallel).
- Totally relax the neck and arms.
- Abdominals are tight the entire time.
- Do not arch the back.
- Keep head between shoulders the entire time.
- Do not allow the head to move forward.
- Start by shrugging shoulders up, and then roll them forward, then down, and then back. This is one complete roll forward and takes 2 counts.
- Now we will do shoulder isolations forward rolls as listed on the warm-up chart. Count silently to yourself as I count. [Do this slowly with students a couple times and give corrections. Do 4 shoulder rolls forward in 2 slow counts each for a total of 8 slow counts.]

Rib Isolations Right to Left
Ribs move right and left 4 times each, total of 8 slow counts

Note: Some students will have difficulty trying to isolate ribs. Many will move shoulders or hips with their ribs, or they will tilt the upper body. Tell students that it is hard to do this isolation, but with practice and concentration they will be able to do this exercise. If some students are having extreme difficulty with this isolation, have them sit on the floor to keep hips from moving.

- Feet are parallel and shoulder-width apart (second position parallel).
- Totally relax the neck and shoulders.
- Abdominals are tight the entire time.
- Do not arch the back.

- Shoulders and hips should remain stationary.
- Do not tilt the shoulders or swing hips.
- Lift the diaphragm.
- Start by putting hands on ribs. Move only the ribs to the right and then to the left for 8 counts.
- Now we will do rib isolations right and left as listed on the warm-up chart. Count silently to yourself as I count. [Do this slowly with students a couple times and give corrections. Move ribs right and left 4 times each for a total of 8 slow counts.]

Rib Isolations Front to Back
Ribs move front and back 4 times each, total of 8 slow counts

- Feet are parallel and shoulder-width apart (second position parallel).
- Totally relax the neck and shoulders.
- Abdominals are tight the entire time.
- Do not arch the back.
- Shoulders and hips should remain stationary.
- Do not tilt the shoulders or swing hips.
- Lift the diaphragm.
- Start by putting hands on ribs. Move only the ribs to the front and then to the back for 8 counts.
- Now we will do rib isolations front and back as listed on the warm-up chart. Count silently to yourself as I count. [Do this slowly with students a couple times and give corrections. Move ribs front and back 4 times each for a total of 8 slow counts.]

Rib Isolations Left to Right
Ribs move left and right 4 times each for a total of 8 slow counts

- Feet are parallel and shoulder width apart (second position parallel).
- Totally relax the neck and shoulders.
- Abdominals are tight the entire time.
- Do not arch the back.
- Shoulders and hips should remain stationary.
- Do not tilt the shoulders or swing hips.
- Lift the diaphragm.
- Start by putting hands on ribs, move only the ribs to the left and then to the right for 8 counts.
- Now we will do rib isolations right and left as listed on the warm-up chart. Count silently to yourself as I count. [Do this slowly with students a couple times and give corrections. Move ribs left and right 4 times each for a total of 8 slow counts.]

Rib Isolations Back to Front

Ribs move back and front 4 times each, total of 8 slow counts

- Feet are parallel and shoulder-width apart (second position parallel).
- Totally relax the neck and shoulders.
- Abdominals are tight the entire time.
- Do not arch the back.
- Shoulders and hips should remain stationary.
- Do not tilt the shoulders or swing hips.
- Lift the diaphragm.
- Start by putting hands on ribs. Move only the ribs to the back and then to the front for 8 counts.
- Now we will do rib isolations back and front as listed on the warm-up chart. Count silently to yourself as I count. [Do this slowly with students a couple times and give corrections. Move ribs back and front 4 times each for a total of 8 slow counts.]

Rib Isolation Circles Right and Left

Right to left for 8 slow counts, then left to right for 8 slow counts, total of 16 slow counts

- Feet are parallel and shoulder-width apart (second position parallel).
- Totally relax the neck and shoulders.
- Abdominals are tight the entire time.
- Do not arch the back.
- Shoulders and hips should remain stationary.
- Do not tilt the shoulders or swing hips.
- Lift the diaphragm.
- Start with hands on ribs. Move only ribs to the right, then take them back, then move them to the left, and then front.
- Reverse by moving only the ribs to the left, and then take them back, then right, and then front.
- Each circle takes 8 counts and should be smooth.
- Now we will do rib isolation circles right and left as listed on the warm-up chart. Count silently to yourself as I count. [Do this slowly with students a couple times and give corrections. Move right to left for 8 slow counts, then left to right for 8 slow counts, for a total of 16 slow counts.]

Reaches Up Right and Left

Alternate reaching up right and left 4 times, 2 counts for each reach, total of 16 counts

- Feet are parallel and shoulder-width apart (second position parallel).
- Keep opposite shoulder down when reaching.

- Do not arch back.
- Reach the arms up so the hands are slightly in front of the shoulders.
- Step on same foot as reaching arm for each reach.
- Abdominals are tight the entire time.
- Arms should be as long as possible when reaching with jazz hands.
- Now we will reach up right and left as listed on the warm-up chart. Count silently to yourself as I count. [Do this slowly with students a couple times and give corrections. Alternate reaching right and left 4 times, 2 counts for each reach, for a total of 16 counts.]

Side Reaches Right and Left

Alternate reaching out to the side right and left 4 times, 2 counts for each reach, total of 16 counts

- Feet are parallel and shoulder-width apart (second position parallel).
- Keep opposite shoulder down when reaching.
- Do not arch back.
- Abdominals are tight the entire time.
- Arms should reach slightly in front of the shoulders, not directly out to the sides.
- Step on the same foot as reaching arm for each reach.
- Arms should be as long as possible when reaching with jazz hands.
- Now we will do side reach right and left as listed on the warm-up chart. Count silently to yourself as I count. [Do this slowly with students a couple times and give corrections. Alternate reaching out to the side right and left 4 times, 2 counts for each reach, for a total of 16 counts.]

Floor Reaches Right and Left

Alternate reaching to the floor right and left 4 times, 2 counts for each reach, total of 16 counts

- Feet are parallel and shoulder-width apart (second position parallel).
- Keep opposite shoulder down when reaching.
- Do not arch back.
- Abdominals are tight the entire time.
- Arms should reach slightly in front of the feet, not directly out to the sides.
- Step on the same foot as reaching arm for each reach.
- Try to touch the floor when reaching.
- Arms should be as long as possible when reaching with jazz hands.
- Now we will do floor reach right and left as listed on the warm-up chart. Count silently to yourself as I count. [Do this slowly with students a couple times and give corrections. Alternate reaching to the floor right and left 4 times, 2 counts for each reach, for a total of 16 counts.]

Side Reaches Right and Left
Alternate reaching out to the side right and left 4 times, 2 counts for each reach, total of 16 counts

Note: This is the same as previous side reach right and left.

- Feet are parallel and shoulder-width apart (second position parallel).
- Keep opposite shoulder down when reaching.
- Do not arch back.
- Abdominals are tight the entire time.
- Arms should reach slightly in front of the shoulders, not directly out to the sides.
- Step on the same foot as reaching arm for each reach.
- Arms should be as long as possible when reaching with jazz hands.
- Now we will do side reach right and left as listed on the warm-up chart. Count silently to yourself as I count. [Do this slowly with students a couple times and give corrections. Alternate reaching out to the side right and left 4 times, 2 counts for each reach, for a total of 16 counts.]

Transition to Floor
4 slow counts

- Turn and face stage right.
- Quickly lie down and get into crunch position.
- Your left side should be toward the audience so that you can see me and so I can monitor your technique.
- Now we will transition to floor as listed on the warm-up chart. Count silently to yourself as I count. [Do this slowly with students a couple times and give corrections. Do it in 4 slow counts.]

Crunches
32 crunches, 1 slow count each, total of 32 slow counts

Note: Some students may not be able to do all of the crunches the first time they try it. Encourage students to work up to doing 32 crunches. If any student needs to take a break during the 32, tell the student to hold the navel down to the floor to at least activate the abs while resting. **Do not decrease the number of crunches.**

- Feet are shoulder-width apart.
- Knees are bent, and feet are flat on floor.
- Hands are either at sides or on the base of the skull, not on the neck; elbows should be held still and not "flap," which pulls on the neck and strains the neck and upper back.
- Chin is tucked to chest gently to help round the back.
- Curl up until shoulder blades are off the floor—no higher.

- Curl back down.
- The back stays rounded the entire time—no flat backs.
- The navel stays "snapped" to the floor the entire time.
- Now we will do crunches as listed on the warm-up chart. Count silently to yourself as I count. [Do this slowly with students a couple times and give corrections. Do 32 crunches, 1 slow count each, for a total of 32 slow counts.]

Oblique Crunches
16 right, then 16 left, 1 slow count each, total of 32 slow counts

Note: Some students might not be able to do all of the crunches the first time they try this exercise. Encourage students to work up to doing 32 crunches. If any student needs to take a break during the 32, tell that student to hold the navel down to the floor to at least activate the abs while resting. **Do not decrease the number of crunches.**

- Use the same position and rules as for crunches.
- Curl up and twist 16 times to opposite knee (or 2 o'clock) until lower shoulder blade is just off the floor.
- Curl up and twist 16 times to opposite knee (or 10 o'clock) until lower shoulder blade is just off the floor.
- Keep both hips flat on floor.
- Keep the navel "snapped" to the floor.
- Now we will do oblique crunches as listed on the warm-up chart. Count silently to yourself as I count. [Do this slowly with students a couple times and give corrections. Do 16 right, then 16 left, 1 slow count each, for a total of 32 slow counts.]

Leg-Out Crunches
16 right, then 16 left, 1 slow count each, total of 32 slow counts

Note: Butt-ups may be substituted for leg-out crunches. If butt-ups are done, the legs are in the air perpendicular to the floor and crossed at the ankles with knees slightly bent. The legs do not move. The butt is lifted off the floor only 1 inch. The arms, shoulders, and neck should not be involved in the movement.

Note: Some students might not be able to do all of the crunches or butt-ups the first time the try it. Encourage students to work up to doing 32. If any student needs to take a break during the 32, tell the student to hold the navel down to the floor to at least activate the abs while resting. **Do not decrease the number of crunches.**

- Follow the same rules as for crunches.
- One knee is bent and the other leg is held straight out and off the floor about 6 inches *only*—no higher.
- Curl up until shoulder blades are just off the floor, as with regular crunches.
- Keep the navel "snapped" to the floor.

- Now we will do leg-out crunches (or butt-ups) as listed on the warm-up chart. Count silently to yourself as I count. [Do this slowly with students a couple times and give corrections. Do 16 right, then 16 left, 1 slow count each, for a total of 32 slow counts.]

Hug Knees to Chest

Hold for 16 slow counts

- Relax, lie on back, and hug knees to chest. This relieves any tension put on the back during crunches.
- Keep the back of the hips on the floor and let the arms do the hugging work.
- Now we will hug knees to chest as listed on the warm-up chart. Count silently to yourself as I count. [Do this slowly with students a couple times and give corrections. Hold for 16 slow counts.]

Transition to Butterfly

4 slow counts

- Release knees from hug.
- Sit up tall, facing the audience. Soles of feet are together.
- Place hands on ankles. Do not hold toes—holding the toes overstretches the outside of the foot and ankle, which makes you more prone to injury.
- Now we will transition to butterfly as listed on the warm-up chart. Count silently to yourself as I count. [Do this slowly with students a couple times and give corrections. Do this in 4 slow counts.]

Butterfly Stretch

Hold for 16 slow counts

Note: Some inflexible students will also feel this in the neck and upper back. These students need to relax by shaking their heads yes and no while holding the stretch.

- Sit up tall, facing audience.
- Put soles of feet together.
- Hold the ankles, *never* the toes.
- Relax the entire body.
- Roll down, head first, and hold.
- You should feel this stretch in the groin.
- Do not force the stretch by straining, pulling, or pushing; let gravity do the work.
- Now we'll do butterfly stretch as listed on the warm-up chart. Count silently to yourself as I count. [Do this slowly with students a couple times and give corrections. Hold for 16 slow counts.]

Transition to Pike Stretch

4 slow counts

- At the end of the butterfly stretch, roll up, starting with lower back and finishing with the head.
- Stretch legs toward audience with knees and feet together (first position parallel).
- Now we will transition to pike stretch as listed on the warm-up chart. Count silently to yourself as I count. [Do this slowly with students a couple times and give corrections. Do this in 4 slow counts.]

Pike Stretch

Hold for 16 slow counts

Note: Some inflexible students will only be able to put the chin on the chest. They might also need to bend the knees to sit up straight to do this. Encourage practice. Students can check to see if their heads are relaxed by shaking their heads yes and no while holding the stretch.

- Arms, shoulders, and head are relaxed. Hands are on thighs (more flexible students can grasp ankles or toes).
- Knees are straight (first position parallel).
- Feet are relaxed (flexible students can flex feet for better stretch).
- Roll down, head first, and hold.
- Totally relax.
- Do not force the stretch by straining, pulling, or pushing; let gravity do the work.
- Now we will do pike stretch as listed on the warm-up chart. Count silently to yourself as I count. [Do this slowly with students a couple times and give corrections. Hold for 16 slow counts.]

Transition to Straddle Stretch

4 slow counts

- At the end of the pike stretch, roll up, starting with lower back and finishing with the head.
- Stretch legs out in a V as wide as is comfortable. Knees and toes face the ceiling.
- Now we will transition to straddle stretch as listed on the warm-up chart. Count silently to yourself as I count. [Do this slowly with students a couple times and give corrections. Do this in 4 slow counts.]

Straddle Stretch

Hold for 16 slow counts

Note: Some inflexible students will not be able to sit up straight in a straddle. They can bend their knees so they can curl the head down a little. Encourage them to relax. It will get better with practice.

- Arms, shoulders, and head are relaxed.
- Make sure you are sitting on two sit bones—rock back and forth to make sure. If you only feel one bone, you are sitting on the bottom of the spine (coccyx). Bend your knees a little and check again by rocking.
- Knees and toes face the ceiling the entire time.
- Feet are relaxed (flexible students can flex feet for a better stretch).
- Roll down, head first, and hold.
- Totally relax.
- Roll up, starting with the lower back and finishing with the head.
- Do not force the stretch by straining, pulling, or pushing; let gravity do the work.
- Now we will do straddle stretch as listed on the warm-up chart. Count silently to yourself as I count. [Do this slowly with students a couple times and give corrections. Hold for 16 slow counts.]

Transition to Low Lunge

4 slow counts

- From straddle stretch, slide legs together.
- Pull knees to chest to tuck into a ball.
- Face stage right.
- Step on right foot and walk left foot back so there is a right angle at the right knee.
- Hands are inside the right knee; lean on the hands.
- Try to keep left leg straight.
- Now we will transition to lunge as listed on the warm-up chart. Count silently to yourself as I count. [Do this slowly with students a couple times and give corrections. Do it in 4 slow counts.]

Low Lunge Right and Left

8 slow counts right, 8 slow counts with right arm up, 8 slow counts left, 8 slow counts with left arm up, total of 32 counts

- Relax head and neck.
- Place weight on hands and right foot.
- Hang with relaxed head, arms, and shoulders.
- Gently press both hips evenly toward floor.
- Try to have a straight line between left foot and right knee.
- Do not strain; let gravity do the work.
- You should feel this stretch in the hip flexor.
- Hold for 8 slow counts.
- Then raise right jazz hand to ceiling and look up at right hand; hold for 8 slow counts.

- Quickly switch to left lunge facing stage left to repeat stretch on left side.
- Now we will do low lunge as listed on the warm-up chart. Count silently to yourself as I count. [Do this slowly with students a couple times and give corrections. Hold for 8 slow counts in each position (plain and hand raised) for a total of 32 counts.]

Transition to Parallel Second
4 slow counts

- Walk the feet up to parallel second, facing the audience.
- Keep the head down so you are inverted.
- Place the weight equally on both feet and on the whole foot.
- Now we will transition to parallel second as listed on the warm-up chart. Count silently to yourself as I count. [Do this slowly with students a couple times and give corrections. Do it in 4 slow counts.]

Plié and Straighten
8 slow counts each, 4 times, total of 32 counts

- Keeping the top of the head facing the floor, bend knees slowly for 4 slow counts.
- Make sure the knees go right out over the toes.
- Keeping the top of the head facing the floor, straighten knees slowly for 4 slow counts.
- This is 1 plié and stretch. We will do this 4 times.
- Place the weight equally on both feet and on the whole foot the entire time.
- Now we will do plié and straighten as listed on the warm-up chart. Count silently to yourself as I count. [Do this slowly with students a couple times and give corrections. Do it 4 times in 8 slow counts each for a total of 32 counts.]

Roll Up
8 slow counts

- This is 8 counts, done smoothly.
- Butt leads the way up, then lower back, then upper back, then neck, then head.
- Abdominal muscles pull you up.
- Now we will roll up as listed on the warm-up chart. Count silently to yourself as I count. [Do this slowly with students a couple times and give corrections. Do it in 8 slow counts.]

You have done a good job learning the movements for our jazz dance warm-up. It might seem that the warm-up is long. Actually, once we do it without any breaks to music, it's not long at all. Does anyone have any questions about the warm-up technique? [Answer any questions.]

Now we will do the warm-up to music. We will make mistakes at first, but that's okay. Just keep trying. You are in charge of your own warm-up. At first, some of the warm-up might be hard for you, but the goal is to work on it until you are able to do all parts correctly and completely and on the counts in the music. If you make a mistake, keep going and don't worry. Practice makes perfect! Your goal is to be ready for the next exercise so you start each new exercise on the count of 1. [Practice the whole warm-up a couple of times and give corrections.]

CLOSURE

- Did you accomplish the outcomes for the lesson?

- What was hard and what was easy?

- For the next class, you will need to memorize the order of the warm-up. I expect to see a big improvement during each lesson!

- Practice difficult parts of the warm-up at home.

- Put your Jazz Dance Warm-Up Chart and Rules for Safe Stretching in your notebooks (or folders).

- Tomorrow you will learn how to go across the floor for the second part of a jazz dance class.

- I'm handing out the Jazz Dance Collage and Homework Essay and the Jazz Dance Collage and Homework Essay Rubric now. [Hand out this form and go over the assignment. Assign the due date for the collage and essay.]

JAZZ DANCE COLLAGE AND HOMEWORK ESSAY

WHY PEOPLE DANCE

COLLAGE

Create a dance collage showing people dancing in a variety of circumstances. Using various media (such as magazines, clip art, photos, Internet), gather pictures of people from various cultures dancing. All pictures should be attached securely with glue.

Your collage should be neat in appearance. Put your name, the date, and the class on the back of your collage.

ESSAY

Research why people from various cultures dance. Write an essay titled "Why People Dance." The title should be at the top of the page. The essay should begin with an introduction, contain paragraphs about why people dance, and end with a summary. The paragraphs should have correct spelling, correct grammar, complete sentences, and correct punctuation. Write the essay on lined paper with black ink or type it using good form in black ink. Handwriting must be neat and legible. Use 12-point font for typed work.

Required size of dance collage: _____

Dance collage due date: _____

Essay due date: _____

From J. Fey, 2011, *Dance units for middle school* (Champaign, IL: Human Kinetics).

JAZZ DANCE COLLAGE AND HOMEWORK ESSAY RUBRIC

Name_____ Class_____

Item	Possible points	Points earned
Collage: neat, correct size		
Collage: variety of pictures	40	
Essay: introduction	10	
Essay: Why People Dance	5	
Essay: correct spelling	20	
Essay: correct grammar	5	
Essay: correct punctuation	5	
Essay: neat, legible, black ink	5	
Total	10	
	100	

From J. Fey, 2011, *Dance units for middle school* (Champaign, IL: Human Kinetics).

JAZZ DANCE COLLAGE AND HOMEWORK ESSAY RUBRIC

Name_____ Class_____

Item	Possible points	Points earned
Collage: neat, correct size		
Collage: variety of pictures	40	
Essay: introduction	10	
Essay: Why People Dance	5	
Essay: correct spelling	20	
Essay: correct grammar	5	
Essay: correct punctuation	5	
Essay: neat, legible, black ink	5	
Total	10	
	100	

From J. Fey, 2011, *Dance units for middle school* (Champaign, IL: Human Kinetics).

EXTENSION

- Have dancers research famous jazz dancers and choreographers and report on them. Suggestions are Frankie Manning (Lindy hop), Luigi (original name Eugene Louis Faccuito), Katherine Dunham, Lester Horton, Jack Cole, Eddy Ocampo, Joe Tremaine, Alvin Ailey, Joe Driscoll, Cholly Atkins, Al Gilbert, Matt Mattox, Claude Thompson, Mia Michaels, Joe Lanteri, Joe Orlando, June Taylor, Bob Fosse, Gus Giordano. There are many others. An Internet search using the words "famous jazz dancers" yields many names.

HISTORY OF DANCE

Since ancient times, people have been creative and danced. The rudiments of cave men and women, the ceremonial dances of Roman and Greek society, the cultural dances of just about every country, the desire of royalty to show off, the refinement of steps, the training of classical ballet, the development of notation and preservation, the development of many styles of modern dance, the evolution of contemporary styles of dance found all over the world, the current blending of styles, and the use of technology are all part of the rich history of dance. Efforts are being made, with the help of notation, video, and other technologies, to preserve as much of dance's history as possible. The book *History of Dance* by Gayle Kassing (2007, Human Kinetics) is a wonderful compilation of dance history that is useful as a resource for the dance lessons in this book.

The first dances were created for specific purposes—among them dances to ask for successful crops, to help a couple with fertility, to celebrate through village ceremonies, to maintain the fitness needed for survival, to compete with other villages, and to entertain one another at village events. Part of the dancing was the music. Villagers played instruments and sang to accompany the dances. Dance involved the whole community and was a vital part of community life given that any entertainment had to be created from what crude resources were available in the village.

As societies became more sophisticated, so did their dancing. Refinements like costumes, makeup, specific steps with names, and names for the dances were made, and they were passed through generations. Dance teachers came about, teaching and refining the steps for accurate performance. It was important that dancers showed their prowess in dances. Showing off or performing was part of the fun and gave the performers prestige.

In European courts, elaborate and weighty costumes meant that the steps were limited by costume restrictions and were very strenuous. Men performed elaborate dance shows in the courts, which were A-list events. Dance teachers were held in high regard. This was the beginning of what we know today as classical ballet.

From J. Fey, 2011, *Dance units for middle school* (Champaign, IL: Human Kinetics).   1

- Have dancers research jazz dance companies and report on them. Suggestions are Hubbard Street Dance Chicago, Savage Jazz Dance Company, Alvin Ailey Dance Theater, Dancin' Unlimited, Gravity Dance Company, Gus Giordano Jazz Dance Chicago, Parsons Dance, Columbia City Jazz Dance Company. An Internet search using the words "professional jazz dance companies" will yield more.

- Have dancers use the History of Dance handout as a springboard for researching a period of dance history, dances of a specific culture (possibly what is being studied in social studies class), a dancer from a specific historic period, a well-known dance company with a long history, and so on.

2

WARM-UP, ACROSS THE FLOOR, COMBINATION

OUTCOMES

- Students will perform the jazz warm-up to improve their level of fitness.
- Students will learn stage directions.
- Students will learn appropriate audience etiquette.
- Students will become familiar with across-the-floor patterns in jazz dance.
- Students will perform a variety of locomotor and nonlocomotor movements to music.

NATIONAL DANCE STANDARDS

- Identifying and demonstrating movement elements and skills in performing dance
- Applying and demonstrating critical-thinking and creative-thinking skills in dance
- Making connections between dance and healthful living
- Making connections between dance and other disciplines

MATERIALS

- Music player with enough volume for teaching space
 - Music with steady beat and appropriate lyrics (accompanying CD or see suggestions on page xxiii)
- Projector (overhead or LCD) and computer or dry-erase board
 - Stage Direction signs (if not already posted)
 - Origin of Stage Directions handout
 - Pathways Across the Floor handout

PREPARATION

- Select music to be used during class. Post selections.
 - Post stage direction signs in class space, if signs are not still up from lesson 1. (Audience is downstage.)

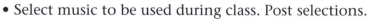

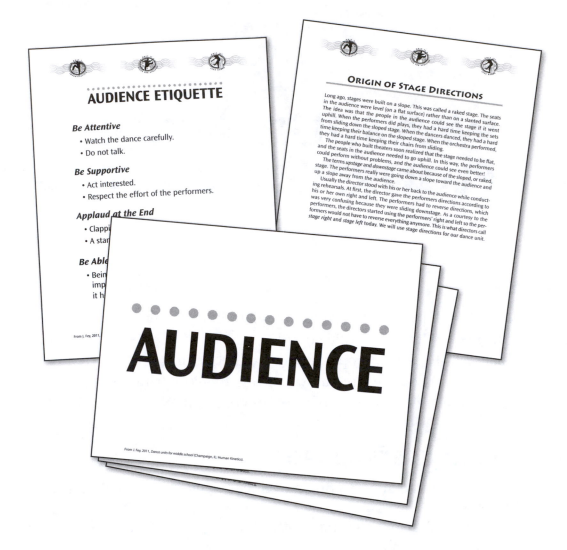

AUDIENCE ETIQUETTE

Be Attentive
- Watch the dance carefully.
- Do not talk.

Be Supportive
- Act interested.
- Respect the effort of the performers.

Applaud at the End
- Clappi
- A star

Be Able
- Bein
  imp
  it h

From J. Fey, 2011,

ORIGIN OF STAGE DIRECTIONS

Long ago, stages were built on a slope. This was called a raked stage. The seats in the audience were level (on a flat surface) rather than on a slanted surface. The idea was that the people in the audience could see the stage if it went uphill. When the performers did plays, they had a hard time keeping the sets from sliding down the sloped stage. When the dancers danced, they had a hard time keeping their balance on the sloped stage. When the orchestra performed, they had a hard time keeping their chairs from sliding.

The people who built theaters soon realized that the stage needed to be flat, and the seats in the audience needed to go uphill. In this way, the performers could perform without problems, and the audience could see even better!

The terms *upstage* and *downstage* came about because of the sloped, or raked, stage. The performers really were going down a slope toward the audience and up a slope away from the audience.

Usually the director stood with his or her back to the audience while conducting rehearsals. At first, the director gave the performers directions according to his or her own right and left. The performers had to reverse directions, which was very confusing because they were sliding downstage. As a courtesy to the performers, the directors started using the performers' right and left so the performers would not have to reverse everything anymore. This is what directors call *stage right and stage left* today. We will use stage directions for our dance unit.

•••••••••••••
AUDIENCE

From J. Fey, 2011, *Dance units for middle school* (Champaign, IL: Human Kinetics).

- Survey class space and determine how to set up across-the-floor movement. Use the Pathways Across the Floor handout to do this.

- Enlarge Pathways Across the Floor and Audience Etiquette to make posters or arrange to project on a wall.

- Run off enough Pathways Across the Floor and Origin of Stage Directions handouts for each student.

- Post Audience Etiquette sign in class space. (Do this early so students see them routinely before they perform.)

- Post outcomes for the lesson.

- Post vocabulary for the lesson.

- Select music for students to use for the jazz dance choreography project. Make CDs of music (one song per CD). This is required for lesson 6 of the unit.

- Predetermine partners and order of partners for going across the floor if students find it hard to move to a new space quickly without becoming disorganized. This will save time.

- Have projector and laptop set up for projecting handouts on a wall.

VOCABULARY

- upstage
- downstage
- stage right
- stage left
- pathway

- jazz walk
- jazz run
- grapevine
- combination

LESSON INTRODUCTION

When students enter the room, seat them in lines (squads) in their warm-up spots facing the audience spread out as far as possible. Ideally, each student would have a 10-foot by 10-foot space.

Audience

X X X X X

X X X X X

X X X X X

X X X X X

X X X X X

Review outcomes for the lesson.

WARM-UP

The warm-up is the same as in lesson 1.

ACROSS THE FLOOR

 If you look around the room, you will see signs posted that say **downstage, upstage, stage right,** and **stage left.** These words are known as stage directions. I will tell you a story about why the stage directions are labeled as they are so that you'll remember them. [Read story from Origin of Stage Directions and go over the signs posted in the room.] We will be using stage directions for our jazz dance unit. At the end of class, you will receive the Origin of Stage Directions to put in your notebook.

In the previous class we learned the warm-up part of jazz class. The next part of class is across the floor. We will learn to count beats, clap beats, walk, run, walk and kick, and grapevine.

 Before we start to work across the floor, let's review the floor pattern. [Project Pathways Across the Floor on a wall.] In this class, two people will move across the floor at the same time. If there is an odd number of students, we will have one group of three. We will start upstage left with the right foot beginning on count 1. Each pair will travel to the downstage-right corner of the stage. Can you see this? [Students answer.] When each pair completes their movement, they will walk to the upstage-right corner and line up again to get ready to do the movement beginning with the left foot. Can you see this? [Students answer.] After everyone in the class has completed the movement from upstage left,

PATHWAYS ACROSS THE FLOOR

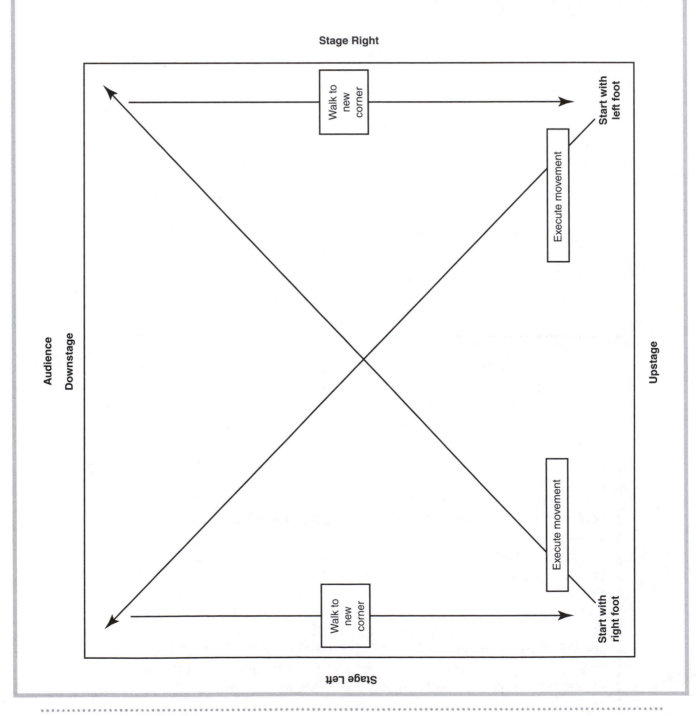

Pathways Across the Floor.

the first group will begin the same movement from upstage right, but this time starting with the left foot on count 1. They will travel to downstage left, then walk to upstage left to get ready for the next movement. The complete **pathway** is similar to a figure 8. Are there any questions about how we travel across the floor? [Answer any questions.] You will receive a Pathways Across the Floor handout at the end of class.

Before we move across the floor, two at a time, let's practice counting to the beat of the music. When you are moving to music, it's important that you stay on the beat of the music. Have you ever seen someone dancing who wasn't moving to the beat of the music? What did it look like? [Possible answers: funny, odd to look at, movement and music did not match, felt weird watching them.] In our jazz dance unit, we will count sets of 8. I'm going to turn on some music and let's all count sets of 8 together to the beat of the music. [Turn on music and practice.]

Now let's clap to the beat of the music. This time I want you to clap on even numbers only. What even numbers will we be dealing with? [Answer is 2, 4, 6, 8. Turn on music and clap to even beats only.] Let's do it again, but this time clap on odd-number counts only. [Turn on music and clap to odd beats only.] Now let's do a challenge and clap only on beats 1, 3, 5, 6, 8. [Do this and any other challenges you want or that students come up with.]

Okay, now that we are all on the same beat, we'll try some movement across the floor. Remember, whenever you start on the upstage-right side of the room, you will start with your left foot on the count of 1; whenever you start at upstage left, you will start with your right foot on the count of 1. You will be going across the floor with your partner, and you will be starting every 8 counts of music. Let's line up in two lines in the upstage-left corner of the room, facing downstage right. Go to your lines without talking! [Students go to lines.]

Note: If students find it hard to move to new spaces quickly, predetermine the partners and their order in line and go over this ahead of time with students.

All skills below are demonstrated on the accompanying DVD, if you would rather use that demonstration than modeling.

I will model the first skill, **jazz walk,** to counts. This walk is done in plié from first position turned out, and the feet are stretched and reaching way out in front. The plié is what allows you to have long, low walks. [Model this skill, counting sets of 8 counts as you walk to the beat.]

I will count the first group in by saying, "5, 6, 7, 8." Then on 1 the first group should begin across the floor with the correct foot (right foot). Everyone should be counting, because the next group will start on the next 1 count. Follow this pattern so that on the count of 1 of every set of 8 counts a new group begins with the correct foot. When you get to the downstage-right corner, line up again, just like you are now, but in the upstage-right corner. Take the pathways we saw on the Pathways Across the Floor diagram. [Put on music, and count the first group in. Groups will follow. Until students get the idea, you might have to count all groups in. Stop the music when all groups have completed walking across the floor.]

Note: It is important for students to learn to count and come in on count 1 without your counting. If you have to count, you cannot give corrections while the students are doing the movement. This may take some practice.

➡ Now we will jazz walk on the beat back from the upstage-right side. This time, step with the left foot on count 1. I will count in the first group with "5, 6, 7, 8." Be sure to count by yourself so that each group starts on the next 1 count. [Put on music and count first group in. Groups will follow. Stop the music when all groups have completed walking across the floor.]

I will model the next skill, jazz walk and clap on every beat, to counts. [Model this skill, counting sets of 8 counts as you walk and clap.]

I will count the first group in by saying, "5, 6, 7, 8." Then on 1 the first group should begin. Everyone should be counting so a new group begins on every 1 count. Be sure to start with your right foot. [Put on music, and count the first group in. Groups will follow.] Repeat walking and clapping back from the stage-right side (start with left foot): "5, 6, 7, 8." [Students start. Stop the music when all groups have completed walking back across the floor.]

Note: To challenge students, have them walk and clap on even numbers, walk on odd numbers, walk backward, or walk sideways with or without clapping.

➡ I will model the next skill, **jazz run,** to counts. The run should be long and low. You should stretch your legs as far as possible. The arms swing in opposition to the legs. [Model the skill, then count the first group in. Remind students to begin with the correct foot. Repeat running back from the stage-right side. Stop the music when all groups have completed walking across the floor.]

Note: Students will want to run faster than the music (like sprinting). If this happens, have the whole class stop and practice running in place on the beat of the music.

Repeat this same procedure for the following skills:

➡ • **Jazz run and clap:** Run on the beat and clap on every beat, on even beats, on odd beats, or specific beats (such as 1, 4, 7, 8).

• **Jazz walk and kick:** Starting from stage left, we will take 3 steps. The first step is on the right foot, the second step is on the left foot, the third step is on the right foot, then kick the left leg. Immediately take three more steps left, right, left, then kick the right leg. The foot must be pointed when it leaves the floor on a kick. The kicking leg is straight—no bent knee. Kick as high as you can with a straight leg. The cue is R, L, R, kick L, L, R, L, kick R. [Count the first group in. Repeat kicking back from stage right. Be sure students step with the left foot first. Stop the music when all groups have done the jazz walk and kick across the floor.]

• **Grapevine from stage left:** Starting from the upstage-left corner, face the side of your right shoulder to the downstage-right corner, where you will finish. Keep your hips facing downstage left. Your arms should be in second position (out to the sides with hands in front of shoulders). Step your right foot to the side, cross your left foot behind your right foot, step your right foot

to the side, cross your left foot in front of your right foot. Each step should be the same size, and all steps keep moving to the downstage-right corner. Repeat. Say this to yourself as you do grapevine: Side, back, side, front, side, back, side, front. [Count the first group in. Stop the music when all groups have completed grapevine across the floor. Once students have the footwork mastered, then have them plié (bend their knees) as they cross their feet.]

- **Grapevine from stage right:** From upstage-right corner, face the side of your left shoulder to the downstage-left corner, where you will finish. Keep your hips facing downstage right. Your arms should be in second position. Step your left foot to the side, cross your right foot behind your left foot, step your left foot to the side, cross your right foot in front. Repeat. [Count the first group in. Stop the music when all groups have completed walking across the floor.]

COMBINATION

 ⟶ The next part of our class is a **combination.** For this, do the jazz walk to your warm-up spots as you were at the beginning of class.

This is the start of our combination. It's important that you practice the combination at home each day because we will be adding a new part to the combination in each lesson.

1. Once music starts, hold for 8 counts.
2. Jazz walk forward (starting with right foot) for 7 counts, and clap on count 8 as you touch your left foot next to the right (touch has no weight).
3. Jazz walk backward (starting with left foot) for 7 counts, and clap on count 8 as you touch the right foot next to the left (touch has no weight).
4. Grapevine to the right for 7 counts. Touch left next to right on 8 and do not put weight on left foot.
5. Grapevine to left for 7 counts. Touch right next to left on 8 and do not put weight on right foot.
6. Jazz run in a big circle clockwise for 8 counts (end up back in your spot): R, L, R, L, R, L, R, L.
7. Hold a pose for 5 seconds. [Stress holding the end position for at least 5 seconds.]

Practice the combination over and over for perfection in the time available. Rotate lines after each couple of practices.

Hints

- Teach the first three steps without music, then with music. Let students practice a couple times.
- Be sure to rotate lines. (The first line should move to the back, then all the other lines move forward one line. Keep repeating until everyone has been in the front line.)
- Teach the next three steps following the same process.

- You may want to call out the steps and counts while dancing and have students do the same.

- You may want to project the combination on the wall or have a poster of it on the wall for students to refer to while practicing.

CLOSURE

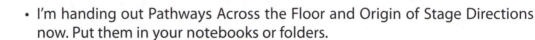

- Did you accomplish the outcomes for the lesson?
- What was hard and what was easy?
- Practice the combination at home so that you can improve.
- Remember the due date for your dance collage and essay.
- I'm handing out Pathways Across the Floor and Origin of Stage Directions now. Put them in your notebooks or folders.

NOTE TO TEACHER

This lesson may take more than one class depending on how quickly students catch on and the length of the class. It is important that students master the work because the skills build. If students cannot do the skills in one class, they will have a difficult time adding the new skills. Technique may not be perfect, but counting sets of 8, coming in on time for across the floor, and doing the skills as best as students can are required before they move on.

EXTENSION

Add arms with jazz hands to the jazz walk forward and backward in the combination (2 and 3) as follows: right arm up (count 1), left arm up (count 2), right arm side (count 3), left arm side (count 4), right arm down (count 5), left arm down (count 6), hold arms down counts on 7 and 8. Use same pattern for forward and back.

3

WARM-UP, ACROSS THE FLOOR, CENTER, COMBINATION

OUTCOMES

- Students will show improvement in the warm-up through memorizing the warm-up and practicing the technique.
- Students will perform a variety of locomotor and nonlocomotor movements to music.
- Students will add to a jazz dance combination.

NATIONAL DANCE STANDARDS

- Identifying and demonstrating movement elements and skills in performing dance
- Applying and demonstrating critical-thinking and creative-thinking skills in dance
- Making connections between dance and healthful living
- Making connections between dance and other disciplines

MATERIALS

- Music player with enough volume for the teaching space

- Music with steady beat and appropriate lyrics (accompanying CD or see suggestions on page xxiii)
- Stage direction signs
- Pathways Across the Floor handout
- Projector (overhead or LCD) and laptop or dry-erase board
- Notebooks or folders for each student and a box to hold them

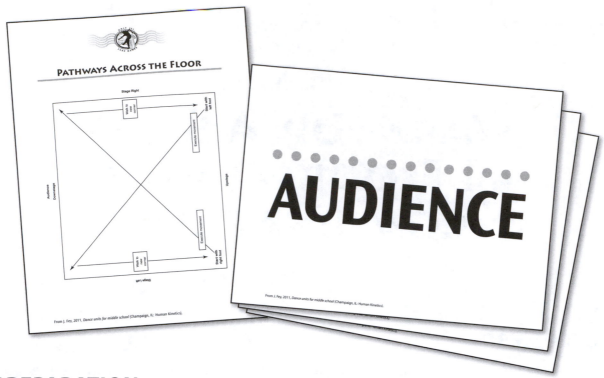

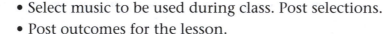

PREPARATION

- Select music to be used during class. Post selections.
- Post outcomes for the lesson.
- Post vocabulary for the lesson.
- Continue to make separate CDs (one song per CD) for students to use for the jazz dance choreography project. This is required for lesson 6 of the unit.

VOCABULARY

- step–together–step–jump and clap
- three-step turn with a touch
- stomp and clap
- paddle turn
- pas de bourrée
- jazz hands

LESSON INTRODUCTION

When students enter the room, seat them in their lines (squads) facing the audience. Review outcomes for the lesson.

WARM-UP

The warm-up is the same as in lesson 1.

ACROSS THE FLOOR

Before we start work across the floor, let's review how we move across the floor. [Project or post Pathways Across the Floor and review.] This is a reminder that two

people will be moving across the floor at the same time. If there is an odd number of students, we will have one group of three.

We will do a quick review. Before we move across the floor, let's first count to the beat of the music. I'm going to turn on some music, and let's all count sets of 8 to the beat of the music. [Turn on music and practice.]

Now let's clap to the beat of the music. This time I want you to clap on even numbers only. [Turn on music and clap on even beats only. Repeat same process, but this time with odd numbers.]

Now that we are all on the same beat, we'll try some movement across the floor. Remember that whenever you start on the stage-right side of the room, you will start with your left foot. Whenever you start on the stage-left side of the room, you will start with your right foot. You will go across the floor two at a time. Which foot will you start on? [Students respond: left foot.]

I will count the first group in by saying, "5, 6, 7, 8," then on 1 the first group should start with the correct foot to go across the floor. The next group should be counting, because they will start on the next 1 count. Follow this pattern.

We will quickly review jazz walk, jazz walk and clap, jazz run, jazz run and clap, jazz walk and kick, and grapevine. [Use procedure from lesson 2, pages 115-117, and run students through these movements. If students have difficulty, stop to model the movement. Review explanations of jazz walk and kick and grapevine, as follows. See lesson 2 for more detailed explanations.]

Jazz Walk and Kick

Starting from stage left, take 3 steps of the jazz walk. The first step is on the right foot, the second step is on the left foot, the third step is on the right foot, and then kick with the left foot. Immediately take 3 more steps; this time start with the left foot and kick with the right foot.

Note: Foot should be pointed when it leaves the floor. The kicking leg is straight—no bent knees.

Grapevine From Stage Left

Starting from stage left, face side of right shoulder to corner of room where you will finish (downstage right). Your arms should be in second position. Step right to the side, cross left foot behind, step right to the side, cross left foot in front. Repeat. Side, back, side, front, side, back, side, front, and so on.

Grapevine From Stage Right

From stage right, face side of left shoulder to corner of room where you will finish (downstage left). Your arms should be in second position. Step left to the side, cross right foot behind, step left to the side, cross right foot in front. Repeat.

CENTER

 Note: Skills are demonstrated on the DVD.

The new part of class for today is center. Come to your warm-up spots to learn today's new skills without music, then with music. The first new skill is **step–together–step–jump and clap.**

Step–Together–Step–Jump and Clap

➡ Start in parallel first position. Step right foot to the side on 1, step left foot together on 2, step right foot to the side on 3, jump both feet together and clap on 4. Change directions. Step left foot to the side on 5, step right foot together on 6, step left foot to the side on 7, jump both feet together and clap on 8. [Turn on music and practice as a class going right and left, forward and backward.]

I will model the next new skill, **three-step turn with a touch,** to counts.

Three-Step Turn With a Touch

➡ Start in parallel first position. The turn is 3 counts. The touch is 1 count. Your arms should be in second position. First, step to the side with your right foot (count 1). Your right foot should be slightly turned out. Next, do a half turn to the right by stepping your left foot over the right foot (count 2). Your body should now face upstage. Then continue to turn right by stepping out to the side with your right foot again (count 3). Your body should face downstage, or the audience. Finally, touch the ball of your left foot on the floor near your right foot (count 4). Make sure the touch does not have weight. Repeat the process to the left. Say to yourself, *Step, step, step, touch.* [Turn on music and practice as a class going right and left.]

Did anyone get dizzy? [Students answer.] Spotting will help. As you turn, keep your eyes focused on a spot on the wall to which you are turning (stage right for turn to the right and stage left for turn to the left) as long as you can. When your body turns, whip your head around and immediately focus on that spot. Let's practice spotting. Stand facing the audience. Keep your eyes on a spot on the audience wall. Begin to turn your body, but keep your eyes on that spot. When you turn so far that you can no longer keep your eyes on the spot, whip your head around as you complete your turn and focus your eyes on that spot again. [Turn on music and practice spotting to both sides several times.]

Note: Some people are natural turners, and spotting comes naturally for them. Others really have to practice to avoid getting dizzy. Encourage practicing at home.

➡ I will model the next new skill, **stomp and clap,** to counts.

Stomp and Clap

➡ Start in parallel first position. Raise your right foot no higher than 6 inches off the floor, and return the foot to the floor with force. Do this movement on the count of 1. Clap on the count of 2 and lift the right foot. Lift the stomp foot as you clap in preparation for the next stomp. The pattern is as follows: stomp R (1), clap (2), stomp R (3), clap (4), stomp R (5), clap (6), stomp R (7), hold (8). Say to yourself, *Stomp, clap, stomp, clap, stomp, clap, stomp, hold.* [Turn on music and practice as a class using right and left feet for the stomp.]

I will model the next new skill, **paddle turn,** to counts.

Paddle Turn Left

➡ Start in parallel first position. Step on the right foot downstage as you turn your body toward stage left. Step on the left foot and turn your body to face upstage. Step on the right foot upstage as you turn your body toward stage right. Step on the left foot and turn your body to face downstage. Notice that the right foot

is the "paddle" for paddle turns to the left. [Turn on music and practice paddle turns to the left.] Which foot do you think will be the paddle for paddle turns to the right? [Students answer.]

Paddle Turn Right

Step on the left foot downstage as you turn your body toward stage right. Step on the right foot and turn your body to face upstage. Step on the left foot upstage as you turn your body toward stage left. Step on the right foot and turn your body to face downstage. Notice that the left foot is the "paddle" for paddle turns to the right. [Turn on music and practice paddle turns to the right.]

I will model the next new skill, **pas de bourrée** (pronounced as PAH-duh-boo-RAY), to counts.

Pas de Bourrée

Start with feet in second position turned out. Step right foot behind left (count 1), step left foot to second position turned out (count 2), then step right foot slightly in front of left (count 3), and hold with weight on the right foot (count 4). We will follow an *up, up, down* pattern. The *up, up* steps are done up on the ball of the foot. Think to yourself, *Up, up, down, hold*, or *Back, side, front, hold*. As we become more proficient with this step, we will increase the speed. [Practice as a class using right and left feet to start the pas de bourrée.] Notice that on the hold on count 4, the back foot is ready to begin pas de bourrée to the other side, so it changes from right to left automatically. Let's practice to music doing back-to-back pas de bourrées. [Turn on music and practice.]

COMBINATION

Now we will add to our combination. Spread out from one another as we did in our previous class. [Be sure to rotate lines.] First we will review the combination from the previous class, and then we will add on new skills. [Note: Numbers 1 to 5 are the review from lesson 2. Numbers 6 to 12 are the new material. Jazz run in a circle is deleted.]

1. Once music starts, hold for 8 counts.
2. Jazz walk forward (starting with right foot) for 7 counts, and clap on count 8 as you touch the left foot next to the right (touch has no weight).
3. Jazz walk backward (starting with left foot) for 7 counts, and clap on count 8 as you touch the right foot next to the left (touch has no weight).
4. Grapevine to the right for 7 counts. Touch left next to right on 8 and do not put weight on left foot.
5. Grapevine to left for 7 counts. Touch right foot next to left on 8 and do not put weight on right foot.
6. Step–together–step–jump and clap. Do right and left (8 counts total; weight is on left foot on count 8).
7. Three-step turn right, left, right, left (16 counts total; weight is on the left foot at the end of the three-step turns).
8. Stomp right (1), clap (2), stomp right (3), clap (4), stomp right (5), clap (6), stomp right (7), hold (8). Say to yourself, *Stomp, clap, stomp, clap, stomp, clap, stomp, hold*.

UNIT III
JAZZ DANCE

9. Stomp left (1), clap (2), stomp left (3), clap (4), stomp left (5), clap (6), stomp left (7), hold (8). Say to yourself, *Stomp, clap, stomp, clap, stomp, clap, stomp, hold.*

10. Paddle turns to the left. Step right, turn upstage, step right, turn downstage, step right, turn upstage, step right, turn downstage (8 counts total; weight is on the left foot at the end of the paddle turns).

11. Pas de bourrée starting with right (back, side, front, hold), pas de bourrée starting with left (back, side, front, hold) (8 counts total; weight will be on the left foot at the end of the pas de bourrées).

12. Hold an end pose for 5 seconds.

Practice combination as a class, rotating lines so each line has a turn downstage.

Hints

- Don't spend too much time trying to perfect what you accomplished in the previous lesson.
- Allow enough time to add on and practice new skills in the combination.
- You may want to call out the steps and counts while dancing, and have students do the same.
- You may want to write the combination on an overhead or board or project it on a wall for students to refer to while practicing.

CLOSURE

- Did you accomplish the outcomes for today?
- What was hard and what was easy?
- Before the next lesson, practice the combination for improvement, and memorize the order of the steps.
- Remember that the next class (lesson 4) is the due date for your dance collage and essay. [Or if the essay and collage are due on a different day, specify the date.]

EXTENSION

Add arms to various movements, as follows:

- Three-step turn: Wrap arms around body while turning. Left arm is in front at end of right turn, right arm is in front at end of left turn.
- Paddle turn: Arms with **jazz hands** (fingers spread wide) go down by the sides of thighs as the paddle foot steps (counts 1 and 3), then bend elbows so that hands are at shoulder height on counts 2 and 4.
- Pas de bourrée: Place jazz hands on back of hips with palms facing upstage.

4

WARM-UP, ACROSS THE FLOOR, CENTER, COMBINATION

OUTCOMES

- Students will show continued improvement in the jazz dance warm-up.
- Students will perform a variety of locomotor and nonlocomotor movements to music.
- Students will show improvement in the jazz dance combination.

NATIONAL DANCE STANDARDS

- Identifying and demonstrating movement elements and skills in performing dance
- Applying and demonstrating critical-thinking and creative-thinking skills in dance
- Making connections between dance and healthful living
- Making connections between dance and other disciplines

MATERIALS

- Music player with enough volume for the teaching space
- Music with a steady beat and appropriate lyrics (accompanying CD or see suggestions on page xxiii)
- Stage direction signs
- Projector (overhead or LCD) and laptop or dry-erase board
- Notebooks or folders for each student and a box to hold them

PREPARATION

- Select music to be used during class. Post selections.
- Post outcomes for the lesson.
- Post vocabulary for the lesson.
- Continue to make separate CDs (one song per CD) for students to use for the jazz dance choreography project. This is required for lesson 6 of this unit.

From J. Fey, 2011, *Dance units for middle school* (Champaign, IL: Human Kinetics).

VOCABULARY

- jazz square
- slide
- sit spin

LESSON INTRODUCTION

When students enter the room, seat them in their lines (squads) facing the audience. Review the outcomes for the lesson.

WARM-UP

The warm-up is the same as in lesson 1.

ACROSS THE FLOOR

➡ Today we will review the locomotor and nonlocomotor movements from our previous class, learn new movements, and add counts to our combination.

Now that we're warmed up, we'll try some moves across the floor. Remember that whenever you start from the upstage-left side of the room, you will start with your right foot. Whenever you start from the upstage-right side of the room, you will start with your left foot. You will go across the floor two at a time and you will start every 8 counts of music, coming in on count 1.

As before, I will count the first group in by saying, "5, 6, 7, 8." Then on count 1 the first group should begin across the floor. The next group should be counting, because they will start on the next 1 count. We follow this pattern for all work across the floor.

Note: Before putting music on, you may want to review more challenging movements from day 3 with students.

➡ We will review jazz walk, jazz walk and clap, jazz run, jazz run and clap, jazz walk and kick, and grapevine across the floor. [Students do this.]

Jazz Walk and Kick

➡ Take 3 steps right, left, right and then kick with the left foot. Immediately take 3 more steps left, right, left and then kick with the right foot. [Students do this.]

Grapevine From Stage Left

➡ Face side of right shoulder to downstage-right corner of room where you will finish. Step right side, cross left foot in back, step right side, cross left foot in front. Repeat. [Students do this.]

Grapevine From Stage Right

➡ Face side of left shoulder to downstage-left corner of room where you will finish. Step left side, cross right foot in back, step left side, cross right foot in front. Repeat. [Students do this.]

CENTER

➡ Do a jazz walk and clap back to your warm-up spot for the center part of class. [Students do this.] Now we will review center movements, including step–together–step–jump and clap, three-step turn with a touch, stomp and clap, paddle turn, and pas de bourrée.

Step–Together–Step–Jump and Clap

➡ First we'll review step–together–step–jump and clap. Start in parallel first position. Step right foot to the side on 1, step left foot together on 2, step right foot to the side on 3, jump both feet together and clap on 4. Change directions. Step left foot to the side on 5, step right foot together on 6, step left foot to the side on 7, jump both feet together and clap on 8. [Turn on music and practice as a class going right and left, forward and backward.]

Three-Step Turn With a Touch

➡ Now let's review the three-step turn. Start in parallel first position. The turn is 3 counts. The touch is 1 count. Your arms should be in second position. First, step to the side with your right foot (count 1). Your right foot should be slightly turned out. Next, do a half turn to the right by stepping your left foot over the right foot (count 2). Your body should now face upstage. Then continue to turn right by stepping out to the side with your right foot again (count 3). Your body should face downstage, or the audience. Finally, touch the ball of your left foot on the floor near your right foot (count 4). Repeat the process to the left. Say to yourself, *Step, step, step, touch.* [Turn on music and practice as a class going right and left.]

Stomp and Clap

➡ Next we'll review stomps. Start in parallel first position. Raise your right foot no higher than 6 inches off the floor, and return the foot to the floor with force. Do this movement on the count of 1. Clap on the count of 2 and lift the right foot. Lift the stomp foot as you clap in preparation for the next stomp. The pattern is as follows: stomp R (1), clap (2), stomp R (3), clap (4), stomp R (5), clap (6), stomp R (7), hold (8). Say to yourself, *Stomp, clap, stomp, clap, stomp, clap, stomp, hold.* [Turn on music and practice as a class using right and left feet for the stomp.]

Paddle Turn Left

➡ Now let's review paddle turn left. Start in parallel first position. Step on the right foot downstage as you turn your body toward stage left. Step on the left foot and turn your body to face upstage. Step on the right foot upstage as you turn your body toward stage right. Step on the left foot and turn your body to face downstage. Notice that the right foot is the "paddle" for paddle turns to the left. [Turn on music and practice paddle turns to the left.] Which foot do you think will be the paddle for paddle turns to the right? [Students answer.]

Paddle Turn Right

➡ Start in parallel first position. Step on the left foot downstage as you turn your body toward stage right. Step on the right foot and turn your body to face upstage. Step on the left foot upstage as you turn your body toward stage left. Step on the right foot and turn your body to face downstage. Notice that the left foot is the "paddle" for paddle turns to the right. [Turn on music and practice paddle turns to the right.]

Pas de Bourrée

➡ Our last review step is pas de bourrée. Start with feet in second position turned out. Step right foot behind left (count 1), step left foot to second turned out (count 2), then step right foot slightly in front of left (count 3), and hold with weight on the right foot (count 4). We will follow an *up, up, down* pattern. The *up, up* steps are done up on the ball of the foot. Think to yourself, *Up, up, down, hold,* or *Back, side, front, hold.* [Turn on music and practice as a class using right and left feet to start the pas de bourrée.]

 Note: Skills are demonstrated on the DVD.

➡   I will model the first new skill, **jazz square,** to counts.

Jazz Square

➡ Start in parallel first position. Step the right foot downstage on count 1, step the left foot across the right on count 2, step the right foot straight back on count 3, step the left foot to the side (stage left) on count 4. This is a jazz square to the right. Notice that the feet made a square. Jazz squares should be done in plié, and the steps should make the largest box possible. Let's do jazz squares to the right to music. Think *Step, cross, back, side.* [Turn on music and practice 8 jazz squares in a row without stopping.] Now we'll do jazz squares to the left. Which foot steps forward? [Students answer *left* and do it.] Which foot crosses over the left? [Students answer *right* and do it.] What comes next? [Students answer *step back with the left foot* and do it.] What is count 4? [Students answer *step right foot to the side (stage right)* and do it.] [Turn on music and practice 8 jazz squares in a row without stopping.]

Note: Practice on one foot until students have the pattern; then change to the other foot.

➡   I will model the next new skill, **slide,** to counts.

Slide

Slides can be done in any direction. There is a leading foot and a trailing foot. The weight goes onto the leading foot. To do more than one slide, the trailing foot pushes off, then the leading foot takes the weight again. Slides are long and low. Let's try it. Start in turned-out first position. Step into a lunge stage right with the right foot (lead foot) on 1. On count 2 step the left foot (trailing foot) across and in front of the right foot and push off with the left foot so the right foot can lunge out to begin another slide. On count 3, step into a lunge stage right. On count 4 push off, and so on, to do a series of slides. The lunges would be on counts 1, 3, 5, and 7. Say to yourself, *Slide, cross, slide, cross, slide,* and so on. [Try this without music several times doing slides right. Once this is mastered, try slides to the left side without music. Then try both sides with music.] Now let's try slides diagonally upstage right and left. [Try this.] Now let's combine right and left slides as follows: 4 right slides to stage right—slide, cross, slide, cross, slide, cross, slide, hold on count 8 (the weight will be on the right foot); then 4 slides to stage left—slide, cross, slide, cross , slide, cross, slide, hold on count 8. [Turn on music and practice this several times.]

I will model the next new skill, **sit spin,** to counts.

Sit Spin

Jump up, swinging your arms over your head, and sit on the floor, bringing your knees to your chest. Lean back slightly to get your feet off the floor and rotate your body in a circle to the right by pushing with the hands. The count is jump up on count 1; get to sitting position on counts 2, 3, 4; and spin on counts 5, 6, 7, 8. [Students do this. Practice to the left also. Once students have mastered this skill, ask for volunteers to show other types of floor turns and have students try them.]

COMBINATION

Now we will work on our **combination.** Spread out from one another as we did in our last class. [Be sure to rotate lines.] First we will review the combination from last class, and then we will add on new skills. [Numbers 1 to 6 are lesson 2; numbers 7 to 11 are lesson 3, and numbers 12 to 14 are the new material. Notice that jazz run in a circle has been deleted.]

1. Once music starts, hold for 8 counts.

2. Jazz walk forward (starting with right foot) for 7 counts, and clap on count 8 as you touch your left foot next to the right (touch has no weight).

3. Jazz walk backward (starting with left foot) for 7 counts, and clap on count 8 as you touch your right foot next to the left (touch has no weight).

4. Grapevine to the right for 7 counts. Touch left next to right on 8 and do not put weight on left foot.

5. Grapevine to the left for 7 counts. Touch right foot next to left foot on 8 and do not put weight on right foot.

6. Step–together–step–jump and clap. Do right and left (8 counts total; weight is on left foot on count 8).

7. Three-step turns right, left, right, left (16 counts total; weight is on the left foot at the end of the three-step turns).

8. Stomp R (1), clap (2), stomp R (3), clap (4), stomp R (5), clap (6), stomp R (7), hold (8). Say to yourself, *Stomp, clap, stomp, clap, stomp, clap, stomp, hold.*

9. Stomp L (1), clap (2), stomp L (3), clap (4), stomp L (5), clap (6), stomp L (7), hold (8). Say to yourself, *Stomp, clap, stomp, clap, stomp, clap, stomp, hold.*

10. Paddle turns to the left. Step right, turn upstage, step right, turn downstage, step right, turn upstage, step right, turn downstage (8 counts total; weight is on the left foot at end of paddle turns).

11. Pas de bourrée starting with right (back, side, front, hold), pas de bourrée starting with left (back, side, front, hold) (8 counts total; weight will be on the left foot at the end of the pas de bourrées).

12. Do 4 jazz squares right (16 counts) ending with weight on left foot. Use jazz hands during the jazz squares: right hand up as right foot steps forward, left hand up as left foot crosses over right, right hand down as right foot steps back, left hand down as left foot steps to the side (stage left).

13. Do 4 right slides diagonally to upstage right (weight ends on right foot), 4 left slides diagonally to upstage left (weight ends on left foot; 16 counts total.

14. Jazz walks right, left, right, kick left to downstage-right corner; then jazz walks left, right, left, kick right to downstage-left corner (8 counts). Arms are in second position for walks and go up to an L opening to the audience for the kicks (right arm up for left kick, left arm up for right kick).

15. Sit spin. Jump up on count 1; get to sitting position on counts 2, 3, 4; sit spin right on counts 5, 6, 7, 8. [Practice combination as a class, rotating lines.]

Hints

- As the combination gets longer, it will take more time to practice. Students will also find it challenging to think ahead about what steps come next.
- Allow enough time to add on and practice new skills in the combination.
- You may want to call out the steps and counts while dancing, and have students do the same.
- You may want to project the combination on a wall for students to refer to while practicing.

CLOSURE

- Did you accomplish the outcomes for the day?
- What was hard and what was easy?
- Now I will collect collages and essays (if this is the due date).
- Memorize the combination because you will not have it up on a wall during your performance.
- Before the next lesson, practice the combination at home so that you can master it.

5

WARM-UP, ACROSS THE FLOOR, CENTER, COMBINATION

OUTCOMES

- Students will perform a variety of dance movements to music.
- Students will show continued improvement in the jazz dance warm-up.
- Students will show continued improvement in the jazz dance combination.

NATIONAL DANCE STANDARDS

- Identifying and demonstrating movement elements and skills in performing dance
- Applying and demonstrating critical-thinking and creative-thinking skills in dance
- Making connections between dance and healthful living
- Making connections between dance and other disciplines

MATERIALS

- Music player with enough volume for the teaching space
- Music with a steady beat and appropriate lyrics (accompanying CD or see suggestions on page xxiii)
- Projector (overhead or LCD) and laptop or dry-erase board
- Notebooks or folders for each student and a box to hold them

PREPARATION

- Select music to be used during class. Post selections.
- Post outcomes for the lesson.
- Post vocabulary for the lesson.
- Continue to make separate CDs (one song per CD) for students to use for the jazz dance choreography project. This is required for lesson 6 of this unit.

VOCABULARY

- chassé
- kick–ball–change
- dig

LESSON INTRODUCTION

When students enter the room, seat them in their lines (squads) facing the audience.

Review the outcomes for the lesson.

WARM-UP

The warm-up is the same as in lesson 1.

ACROSS THE FLOOR

➡ Good warm-up. We are going to learn two new steps today and finish our jazz dance combination! Now let's go across the floor. Line up quickly. [Students do this.] I will count the first group in by saying "5, 6, 7, 8," then on 1 the first group should begin across the floor. The next group should be counting, because they will start on the next 1 count. Follow this pattern for all across-the-floor work. Today we are going to try doing all of the skills without stopping. I'll call them out but we won't stop the music! That means the movement will be continuous and there will be a new group coming in every set of 8 counts. Let's try it. [Students do this. Call out the next movement 8 counts ahead of time for the starting group in the upstage-left corner.]

We will review jazz walk, jazz walk and clap, jazz run, jazz run and clap, jazz walk and kick, grapevine across the floor, step–together–step–jump and clap, and three-step turn with a touch.

Jazz Walk and Kick

➡ Take 3 steps—right, left, right—then kick with the left foot. Immediately take 3 more steps—left, right, left—then kick with the right foot.

Grapevine From Stage Left

➡ Face side of right shoulder to corner of room where you will finish. Step right side, cross left foot in back, step right side, cross left foot in front. Repeat.

Grapevine From Stage Right

➡ Face side of left shoulder to corner of room where you will finish. Step left side, cross right foot in back, step left side, cross right foot in front. Repeat.

CENTER

➡ Do jazz walks with kicks to move to your warm-up spots to practice some other center jazz dance movements. [Students go to warm-up spots.]

Step–Together–Step–Jump and Clap

⮕ Start in parallel first position. Step right foot to the side on 1, step left foot together on 2, step right foot to the side on 3, jump both feet together and clap on 4. Change directions. Step left foot to the side on 5, step right foot together on 6, step left foot to the side on 7, jump both feet together and clap on 8. [Turn on music and practice as a class going right and left, forward and backward.]

Three-Step Turn With a Touch

⮕ Start in parallel first position. The turn is 3 counts. The touch is 1 count. Your arms should be in second position. First, step to the side with your right foot (count 1). Your right foot should be slightly turned out. Next, do a half turn to the right by stepping your left foot over the right foot (count 2). Your body should now face upstage. Then continue to turn right by stepping out to the side with the right foot again (count 3). Your body should face downstage, or the audience. Finally, touch the ball of your left foot on the floor near your right foot (count 4). Repeat the process to the left. Say to yourself, *Step, step, step, touch*. [Turn on music and practice as a class going right and left.]

Stomp and Clap

⮕ Start in parallel first position. Raise your right foot no higher than 6 inches off the floor, and return the foot to the floor with force. Do this movement on the count of 1. Clap on the count of 2 and lift the right foot. Lift the stomp foot as you clap in preparation for the next stomp. The pattern is as follows: stomp R (1), clap (2), stomp R (3), clap (4), stomp R (5), clap (6), stomp R (7), hold (8). Say to yourself, *Stomp, clap, stomp, clap, stomp, clap, stomp, hold*. [Turn on music and practice as a class using right and left feet for the stomp.]

Pas de Bourrée

⮕ Start with feet in second position turned out. Step right foot behind left (count 1), step left foot to second turned out (count 2), then step right foot in place (count 3), and end with feet flat on floor in second position turned out. We will follow an *up, up, down* pattern. The *up, up* steps are done up on the ball of the foot. Think to yourself, *Up, up, down, hold*, or *Back, side, front, hold*. [Practice as a class using right and left feet to start the pas de bourrée.]

Jazz Square

⮕ Start in parallel first position. Cross the right foot over the left foot on 1, step back with the left foot on 2, step to the right with the right foot on 3, tap the left foot next to right on 4, cross the left foot over the right on 5, step back with the right on 6, step to the left with the left foot on 7, jump with both feet together on 8. Repeat starting with the left foot crossing over the right foot on 1. [Practice as a class using right and left to start the jazz square.]

Slide

⮕ Start in turned-out first position. Step into a lunge stage right with the right foot (lead foot) on 1. On count 2 step the left foot (trailing foot) across and in front of

the right foot and push off with the left foot so the right foot can lunge out to begin another slide. On count 3, step into a lunge stage right. On count 4 push off, and so on, to do a series of slides. The lunges would be on counts 1, 3, 5, and 7. Say to yourself, *Slide, cross, slide, cross, slide,* and so on. [Try this without music several times doing slides right. Once this is mastered, try slides to the left side without music. Then try both sides with music.] Now let's try slides diagonally upstage right and left. [Try this.] Now let's combine right and left slides as follows: 4 right slides to stage right—slide, cross, slide, cross, slide, cross, slide, hold on count 8 (the weight will be on the right foot), then 4 slides to stage left—slide, cross, slide, cross , slide, cross, slide, hold on count 8. [Turn on music and practice this several times.]

Sit Spin

Jump up, swinging your arms over your head, and sit on the floor, bringing your knees to your chest. Lean back slightly to get your feet off the floor and rotate your body in a circle to the right by pushing with the hands. The count is jump up on count 1; get to sitting position on counts 2, 3, 4; and spin on counts 5, 6, 7, 8. [Students do this. Practice to the left also. Once students have mastered this skill, ask for volunteers to show other types of floor turns and have students try them.]

 Note: Skills are demonstrated on the DVD.

Now we will learn some new movements. I will model **kick–ball–change** with lunge to counts.

Kick–Ball–Change With Lunge

Kick the right foot out front low to the floor on 1, bring the right foot back and dig the ball of the right foot into the floor behind the left foot on *and* (a **dig** is putting weight lightly on the ball of the foot to change weight), step on the left foot on 2 (change), and repeat for counts 3 and 4, 5 and 6. Lunge to the right on 7, 8, making sure the weight is on the right foot. Saying to yourself, *Kick–ball–change, kick–ball–change, kick–ball–change, lunge,* or counting 1 + 2, 3 + 4, 5 + 6, 7, 8 will help you get the rhythm. Repeat to the left. [Practice as a class, starting with the right and left feet.]

Line up for the next new movement across the floor. I will model **chassé** and leap to counts.

Chassé and Leap

A chassé is step–together–step. In a chassé one foot literally chases the other foot. The rhythm is long, short, long, and the count is *1 and 2.* Start in turned-out first position. Step forward with your right foot on 1. The left foot steps next to the right foot (chasing it) on *and,* then the right foot recovers on 2 by taking another long step. The left foot begins the next chassé on 3, the right foot chases the left on *and,* then the left foot takes another long step on 5. Now do another chassé starting with the right foot (5 + 6). Now leap with the left leg on 7, 8. When you leap you want to jump in the air, reaching your legs straight out with the left leg in front of your body and the right leg behind your body (like doing a split in the air). Point

your feet when in the air. We just did chassé right, chassé left, chassé right, leap left. Let's repeat this several times to make sure we have it. [Practice as a class starting with chassé right. When students seem comfortable, have them go across the floor with the pattern. Then practice from upstage right starting with chassé left, chassé right, chassé left, and leap with the right leg front several times as a class. When students seem comfortable, have them go across the floor with the pattern.]

COMBINATION

Now we will work on our combination. Spread out from one another as we did in our previous class. [Be sure to rotate squads.] First we will review the combination from the previous class, and then we will add on new skills. [Numbers 1 to 6 are lesson 2, numbers 7 to 11 are lesson 3, numbers 12 to 15 are lesson 4, and numbers 16 to 20 are the new material.]

1. Once music starts, hold for 8 counts.
2. Jazz walk forward (starting with right foot) for 7 counts, and clap on count 8 as you touch the left foot next to the right (touch has no weight).
3. Jazz walk backward (starting with left foot) for 7 counts, and clap on count 8 as you touch the right foot next to the left (touch has no weight).
4. Grapevine to the right for 7 counts. Touch left next to right on 8 and do not put weight on left foot.
5. Grapevine to the left for 7 counts. Touch right foot next to left on 8 and do not put weight on right foot.
6. Step–together–step–jump and clap. Do right and left (8 counts total; weight is on left foot on count 8).
7. Three-step turns right, left, right, left (16 counts total; weight is on the left foot at the end of the three-step turns).
8. Stomp right (1), clap (2), stomp right (3), clap (4), stomp right (5), clap (6), stomp right (7), hold (8). Say to yourself, *Stomp, clap, stomp, clap, stomp, clap, stomp, hold.*
9. Stomp left (1), clap (2), stomp left (3), clap (4), stomp left (5), clap (6), stomp left (7), hold (8). Say to yourself, *Stomp, clap, stomp, clap, stomp, clap, stomp, hold.*
10. Paddle turns to the left. Step right, turn upstage, step right, turn downstage, step right, turn upstage, step right, turn downstage (8 counts total; weight is on the left foot at end of paddle turns).
11. Pas de bourrée starting with right (back, side, front, hold), pas de bourrée starting with left (back, side, front, hold) (8 counts total; weight will be on the left foot at the end of the pas de bourrées).
12. Do 4 jazz squares right (16 counts) ending with weight on left foot. Use jazz hands during the jazz squares: right hand up as right foot steps forward, left hand up as left foot crosses over right, right hand down as right foot steps back, left hand down as left foot steps to the side (stage left).
13. Do 4 right slides diagonally to upstage right (weight ends on right foot), 4 left slides diagonally to upstage left (weight ends on left foot; 16 counts total).
14. Jazz walks right, left, right, kick left to downstage-right corner; then jazz walks left, right, left, kick right to downstage-left corner (8 counts). Arms are in second position for walks

and go up to an L opening to the audience for the kicks (right arm up for left kick, left arm up for right kick).

15. Sit spin. Jump up on count 1; get to sitting position on counts 2, 3, 4; sit spin right on counts 5, 6, 7, 8.

16. Cross right leg over left leg and stand up without using hands; end in second position parallel facing upstage (counts 1, 2, 3, 4). Jump (called a sauté) in place on count 5, jump and turn left ending in second position parallel facing downstage (audience) on count 7. Hold on count 8.

17. Kick–ball–change with right three times (1 and 2, 3 and 4, 5 and 6) lunge to the right 7, 8. Arms swing naturally on kick–ball–change and reach up over head on lunge.

18. Kick–ball–change with left three times (1 and 2, 3 and 4, 5 and 6) and lunge to the left 7, 8. Arms swing naturally on kick–ball–change and reach up overhead on lunge.

19. Chassé right (1 and 2), chassé left (3 and 4), chassé right (5 and 6), leap left (7 and 8). Arms are in L position at shoulder height on chassé and go up overhead on leap.

20. End with students striking their own poses. Hold pose for 5 seconds. [Practice combination as a class, rotating lines. After a few practices, remove the cues posted on the wall so students have to do the combination from memory. Practice from memory, changing lines.]

Hints

- You may want to call out the steps and counts while dancing, and have students do the same.

- You may want to write the combination on an overhead or board, or project it on a wall for students to refer to while practicing.

- You may want to make large flashcards of the combination with key words and directions. You can hold up the flashcards while students practice.

CLOSURE

- Did you accomplish the outcomes for the lesson?

- What was hard and what was easy?

- Continue to practice the combination for improvement.

- At the next class, you will work on choreographing a dance (the choreographic process). You will be working on your own choreography in groups for your final assessment.

- Select two pieces of music used during class that you might want to use for your dance. Everyone in your group must agree on the music being used. You will give your music selections to me by the end of the next class after you have worked in your groups.

- Remember to bring a pencil to the next class.

EXTENSION

- The combination can be done in canon. Divide the class into groups and have students create an 8-count entrance and an 8-count exit for their group that will get their group to a spread-out formation in the center of the performance area. As the first group exits, the second group enters and does the combination, then the third group goes, and so on. One group is exiting at the same time the next group is entering. Groups will have to coordinate so they do not collide.

- Students can rehearse the combination and use it as a performance for any school event. If there is more than one dance class, dancers can audition to perform. If this is known ahead of time, it is motivation for students to learn and dance the combination well.

- Divide into groups and have each group choreograph their own 8-count ending.

- Divide into four groups. Have one group watch while the other three groups perform, but have one group perform facing the audience, another group facing stage right, and the third group facing stage left. Make sure the space is large enough for students to do the traveling movements without colliding. Give each group a chance to watch. Then ask students how it looked and what they could do to enhance it. Try some of the changes they suggest.

JAZZ DANCE
CHOREOGRAPHY PROJECT

OUTCOMES

- Students will identify elements of choreography.
- Students will learn how to use a Pathways Map and a Daily Contribution Sheet.
- Students will develop their own Pathways Maps and Daily Contribution Sheets based on their choreography.
- Students will work cooperatively to choreograph a jazz combination for their final assessment.

NATIONAL DANCE STANDARDS

- Identifying and demonstrating movement elements and skills in performing dance
- Understanding choreographic principles, processes, and structures
- Understanding dance as a way to create and communicate meaning
- Applying and demonstrating critical-thinking and creative-thinking skills in dance
- Making connections between dance and healthful living
- Making connections between dance and other disciplines

MATERIALS

- Music player with enough volume for the class space
- Music (CDs made from previous classes)
- Pencils for students who forget to bring them
- Paper clips to clip each group's Pathways Maps and Daily Contribution Sheets together, or use a folder for each group

- Projector and laptop
- One small music player for each project group (students may volunteer to bring these in if they are not available at school)
 • Choreographing a Dance handout
 • Jazz Dance Criteria handout
 • Pathways Map Instructions handout
 • Pathways Map
 • Daily Contribution Sheet
 • Jazz Dance Choreography Project Groups
 • Workstation number signs
 • Bring a Pencil sign

PREPARATION

 • Post outcomes for the lesson.
 • Post vocabulary for the lesson.
 • Post Bring a Pencil sign.
- Make CDs of music used over the course of the unit for students to use during choreography. If two groups want to use the same music, make two copies of the music or let groups work near each another with the same music player.
- Set up and space out music players for groups. Get extension cords if needed. If students bring in music players, label them with students' names and make provisions to store them safely.
 • Laminate and post workstation number signs at music players.
- Set up projector and laptop to project handouts onto a wall (or have large posters made).
 • Decide the method for selecting groups for the project (for example, students select their groups, you preassign groups, draw numbers, and so on). (Use Jazz Dance Choreography Project Groups sheets to keep record.)
- Run off enough Jazz Dance Choreography Project Groups sheets for all students.
 • Post stage direction and audience signs and Audience Etiquette sign if not posted earlier in the unit.
 • Run off enough copies of Choreographing a Dance, Jazz Dance Criteria, Pathways Map Instructions, Pathways Maps, and Daily Contribution Sheets for all students. Note: Put Jazz Dance Criteria on the back of Choreographing a Dance. Put Pathways Map Instructions on the back of Pathways Map. This uses less paper, saves handing-out time, and makes it easier for students.

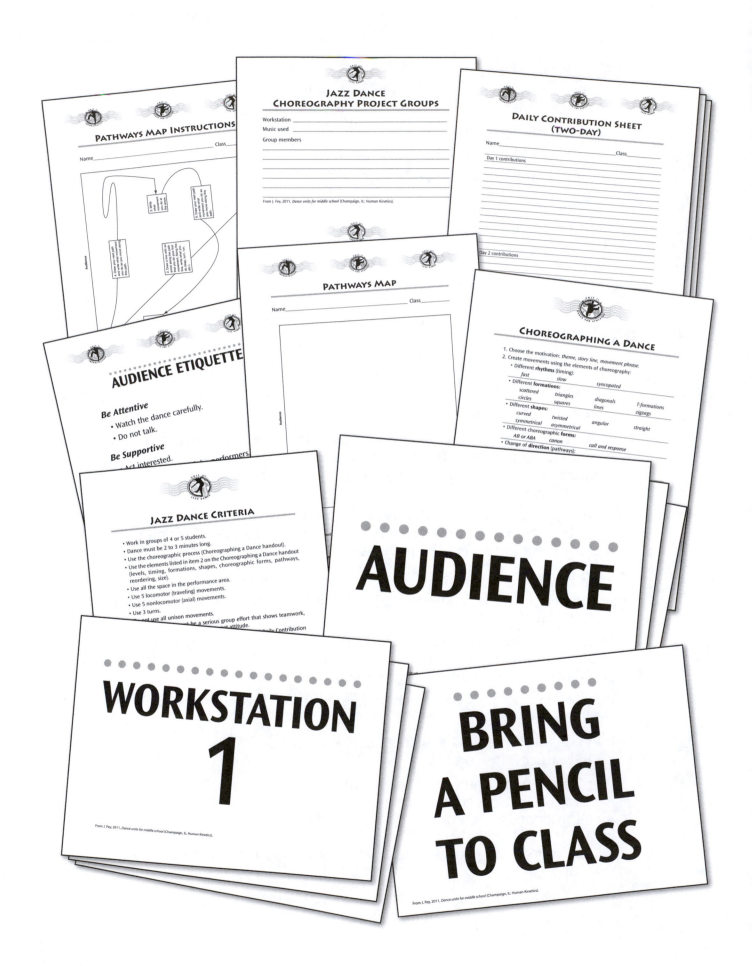

PATHWAYS MAP INSTRUCTIONS

Name_____ Class_____

JAZZ DANCE
CHOREOGRAPHY PROJECT GROUPS

Workstation _____
Music used _____
Group members _____
_____
_____
_____
_____

From J. Fey, 2011, *Dance units for middle school* (Champaign, IL: Human Kinetics).

DAILY CONTRIBUTION SHEET
(TWO-DAY)

Name_____ Class_____

Day 1 contributions

Day 2 contributions

PATHWAYS MAP

Name_____ Class_____

AUDIENCE ETIQUETTE

Be Attentive
• Watch the dance carefully.
• Do not talk.

Be Supportive

CHOREOGRAPHING A DANCE

1. Choose the motivation: *theme, story line, movement phrase.*
2. Create movements using the elements of choreography:
   • Different **rhythms** (timing):
      fast   *slow*   *syncopated*
   • Different **formations:**
      scattered   *triangles*
      circles   *squares*   *diagonals*   *T-formations*
   • Different **shapes:**   *lines*   *zigzags*
      curved   *twisted*
      symmetrical   *asymmetrical*   *angular*   *straight*
   • Different choreographic **forms:**
      AB or ABA   *canon*   *call and response*
   • Change of **direction** (pathways):

JAZZ DANCE CRITERIA

• Work in groups of 4 or 5 students.
• Dance must be 2 to 3 minutes long.
• Use the choreographic process (Choreographing a Dance handout).
• Use the elements listed in item 2 on the Choreographing a Dance handout (levels, timing, formations, shapes, choreographic forms, pathways, reordering, size).
• Use all the space in the performance area.
• Use 5 locomotor (traveling) movements.
• Use 5 nonlocomotor (axial) movements.
• Use 3 turns.
• Do not use all unison movements.   be a serious group effort that shows teamwork,   attitude.   Daily Contribution

AUDIENCE

WORKSTATION
1

From J. Fey, 2011, *Dance units for middle school* (Champaign, IL: Human Kinetics).

BRING
A PENCIL
TO CLASS

From J. Fey, 2011, *Dance units for middle school* (Champaign, IL: Human Kinetics).

VOCABULARY

- Pathways Map
- Daily Contribution Sheet
- syncopated
- scattered
- zigzag
- twisted
- angular
- symmetrical

- asymmetrical
- AB
- ABA
- call and response
- canon
- reordering
- retrograde

LESSON INTRODUCTION

When students enter the room, seat them in warm-up spots facing the audience. Review the outcomes for the lesson.

WARM-UP

The warm-up is the same as in lesson 1.

Note: Across-the-floor, center, and combination work can be omitted for today to give students the maximum amount of time to work in their groups.

➡ Today we will begin our final assessment project. You will be working in groups of four or five. Each group will perform their project for the class. We might invite others to the performances. You will complete a self-assessment for your project and a group assessment of one of the groups in the class after the performances. After the performances, you will write a critique based on a criteria sheet.

You will practice and perform your jazz dance to a piece of music selected by your group. Your homework was to select two pieces of music that we have used in class that you would like to use for your dance. When you get into your group, you will all share your selections and then select one piece of music to use. Everyone in the group needs to agree on the music. This might mean compromising!

Each person will complete a Pathways Map and a Daily Contribution Sheet. I will hand out these sheets and we will go over them. Do not write anything on the sheets until I give instructions. [Pass out Pathways Maps and Pathways Map Instructions. These two handouts should be copied front and back on one sheet of paper. This will reduce the number of papers, and students will be able to simply flip over the paper to refer to the instructions when creating their own maps.]

Now that we all have the first handout, neatly write your name, date, and class period on the paper. Look at the *instructions* for the **Pathways Map.** [Project this on the wall.] This sheet is an example of how someone might do a Pathways Map. This example is *not* for anyone to copy. Look in the lower-right corner of the paper and find the word *start*. When you start working in your group, you will write *start* on your map in the place on the floor where you, personally, start to move. The arrows show the path and direction you move. You will see that the student in the example drew an arrow from 1, *start*, to 3, and wrote along the arrow line, in box 2, what movement she did. Look at 3. In the example, the student wrote the movement that she did in this location. From 3, she took a crazy path to 5. Along the arrow line, in box 4, she wrote the movement she did while traveling along this path. Does everyone understand how to complete a Pathways Map? [Answer any questions.] Keep your Pathways Maps with you, and as your group plans your movement for the project, write your paths and movements on your Pathways Map. Be sure to use pencil, because your Pathways Map might need to change as your group works.

Now we will pass out the Daily Contribution Sheets. [Pass out sheets.] Neatly write your name, date, and class period on this paper. Let's look at the **Daily Contribution Sheet.** [Project this on the wall.] Each day, as you work on your project, write on your Daily Contribution Sheet what you have contributed to the group. Completing the Daily Contribution Sheet completely and accurately is part of the grade for the project, so you want to do a good job. [An example of a contribution might be "I made up the arm movement for our runs."] Does everyone understand how to complete a Daily Contribution Sheet? [Answer any questions.]

I am passing out Choreographing a Dance and Jazz Dance Criteria. Remember to neatly write your name, date, and class period on this paper. [Pass out this handout. These two handouts should be copied front and back on one sheet of paper. This will reduce the amount of paper used and allow students to simply flip over the paper to refer to when creating their dance.] These handouts explain how to create a dance and what your jazz dance must have in it in order for you to earn all possible points. Let's take a minute to look at this handout. [Project these on the wall and discuss contents with class.]

You might need to explain some of the terms on the Steps to Choreographing a Dance handout:

- **Syncopated** is an uneven rhythm, like kick–ball–change (count of "1 *and* 2" rather than even counts).
- **Scattered** means irregular random formation or with no identifiable shape.
- **Zigzag** is a series of diagonals.
- **Twisted** looks like a corkscrew.
- **Angular** means sharp angles of body parts.
- **Symmetrical** is even on both sides (for example, both arms held at the same height or the same number of dancers on both sides of the space).
- **Asymmetrical** is uneven or unbalanced from side to side.
- **AB** is a two-part composition with two distinct self-contained sections; one is called A and the other is called B. The two parts share something, like style, tempo, or movement quality.
- **ABA** is a composition with A and B performed as normal. The second time A is performed, it is changed in some way, such as shorter or longer or abbreviated.
- **Call and response** occurs when a soloist or group performs, then the second soloist or group performs in response to the first.
- **Canon** involves groups performing the same movement beginning at different times. "Row, Row, Row Your Boat" is a canon.
- **Reordering** is changing the order of the counts of a movement.
- **Retrograde** is doing a movement backward (reversing the counts).

When you get into your groups, you will want to refer to the sheets called Choreographing a Dance and Jazz Dance Criteria that we just went over. If you use these sheets as a guide, you will meet all the criteria for your jazz dance.

At the end of each class, everyone will turn in their Pathways Map and Daily Contribution Sheet. If there are no questions, let's get into our groups and begin working. [Either allow students to choose their own groups—giving them no more than 2 minutes to decide—or assign groups ahead of time.] Once you have your group together, come up and I will assign your group a workstation. You will be at this workstation for the rest of the time we are working on our projects. Go to your workstation and have a seat as soon as your workstation is assigned. [Make a list of group members, workstation number, and music used; use Jazz Dance Choreograph Project Groups sheet. You can do this while students are working.]

You will have no more than 2 minutes to decide which music your group will use. One person from your group will come see me, and I will give you a copy of the music. Begin work as soon as you get your music. Work as a group to decide how your group will meet the criteria on the handout given. Make sure the movement you select is appropriate and safe.

Note: Allow students to work in the time remaining. Circulate to monitor and answer questions. List group members, workstation number, and music during this time. Do not tell students how to do the project; they have to figure that out for themselves. Remind groups to complete their Daily Contribution Sheets and Pathways Maps as they work.

CLOSURE

Come over and have a seat. Bring your Pathways Maps, Daily Contribution Sheets, and pencils (if you borrowed one) with you. We made a lot of progress today. Today was the hard part—getting all the instructions and getting started. For the next two classes you will have almost the entire class to work on your project. You will perform your project for the class the following day. At our next class we will go over the rubric for your project. You will also need to bring a pencil with you. Put your Pathways Map, Daily Contribution Sheet, Choreographing a Dance, and Jazz Dance Criteria together. One person in each group will collect them and bring them to me. [Clip the papers from each group together or have a folder for each group or student. This will save time when handing them out on subsequent days.]

- Did you meet your outcomes for the lesson?
- Do you have any questions?
- Would you like to invite others to the performance, such as parents, other teachers, and the principal? (The more people who see and value the program, the better.)

Note: This day will be hectic. Some groups will be confused and need help, especially if they have difficulty deciding on music. Reassure students as you walk around while they work that the next classes will be much easier.

7

JAZZ DANCE CHOREOGRAPHY PROJECT

OUTCOME

Students will work cooperatively to choreograph a jazz combination for their final assessment.

NATIONAL DANCE STANDARDS

- Identifying and demonstrating movement elements and skills in performing dance
- Understanding choreographic principles, processes, and structures
- Understanding dance as a way to create and communicate meaning
- Applying and demonstrating critical and creative thinking skills in dance
- Making connections between dance and healthful living
- Making connections between dance and other disciplines

MATERIALS

- Music player with enough volume for the class space
- Music (CDs made from previous classes)
- Pencils for students who forget to bring them
- Paper clips to clip each group's Pathways Maps and Daily Contribution Sheets together, or use a folder for each group
- Projector and laptop
- One small music player for each project group (students may volunteer to bring these in if they are not available at school)
- Stopwatch for each group
- Workstation number signs
- Jazz Dance Project Rubric
- Bring a Pencil sign

PREPARATION

- Post outcomes for the lesson.
- Post Bring a Pencil sign.

- Have CDs of music that students chose for their group choreography. If two groups are using the same music, make two copies of the music or let groups work near each other with the same music player.

- Set up and space out music players for groups. Get extension cords if needed. If students bring in music players, label them with students' names and make provisions to store them safely.

- Laminate and post workstation number signs at music players.

- Set up projector and laptop to project handouts onto a wall (or have large posters made).

 • Post stage directions and audience signs and Audience Etiquette sign if not previously posted.

 • Run off enough copies of Jazz Dance Project Rubric for all students.

LESSON INTRODUCTION

When students enter the room, seat them in their warm-up spots facing the audience.

Review outcomes for the lesson.

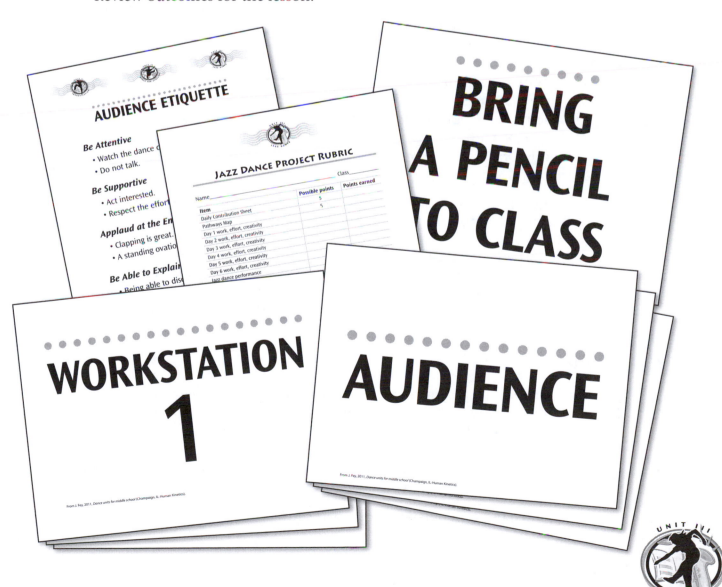

WARM-UP

The warm-up is the same as in lesson 1.

➡ Before we begin working on our projects, we will look at the Jazz Dance Project Rubric. [Pass out Jazz Dance Project Rubric.] As soon as you get your sheet, neatly write your name and class on it.

Follow along with me as we go over the Jazz Dance Project Rubric. This will help you work to get the most points on your project. [Project the Jazz Dance Project Rubric on the wall.] On performance day, each of you will be scored with the use of the rubric. Notice that how you work each day is part of the scoring. Completing your Pathways Map and Daily Contribution Sheet is also part of your score. When you worked yesterday, you saw that there were required elements (movements) on your Jazz Dance Criteria Sheet. Forty points are awarded for including all of these elements in your project. Performance requirements means that your group obviously practiced their project and performed it seriously, with strong movement, and with a very good attitude. You notice that you are also scored on your audience etiquette. That means demonstrating all the items on the audience etiquette signs that have been posted since the second day of our unit. At the bottom of the rubric, notice that points are awarded for completing your self-assessment and group assessment. Does anyone have any questions about the scoring for the project?

In a minute you will move to your group workstations. Once you are with your group, I need one person from the group to collect all the rubrics, bring the rubrics to me, and pick up your Pathways Maps, Daily Contribution Sheets, and a stopwatch so you can time your group's dance to meet the criteria. You should begin work quickly. Don't forget to complete your Pathways Map and Daily Contribution Sheet as you work.

Note: Circulate to monitor students' progress. Remind them that they must work efficiently, because they have only one more day to work. Some groups will get to work and organize their project quickly. Encourage them to practice repeatedly for perfection. Other groups may need motivation. Encourage group work habits, compromise, and selecting a captain if leadership is lacking. Also mention that home practice is necessary so that everyone in the group can do the movements well. Students may ask for more time to work. This will help you decide whether to extend the work days.

CLOSURE

➡ Come over and sit with your group. Be sure to bring your Pathways Maps, Daily Contribution Sheets, and stopwatches with you. Remember to practice at home. Tomorrow is the last day to work on the project in class. If your group needs ideas, talk with parents and friends, and bring ideas back to class. One person in each group needs to collect the Pathways Maps, Daily Contribution Sheets, and stopwatch and turn them in to me.

- Did you meet your outcomes for the lesson?
- Do you have any questions?

JAZZ DANCE CHOREOGRAPHY PROJECT

OUTCOME

Students will work cooperatively to choreograph a jazz combination for their final assessment.

NATIONAL DANCE STANDARDS

- Identifying and demonstrating movement elements and skills in performing dance
- Understanding choreographic principles, processes, and structures
- Understanding dance as a way to create and communicate meaning
- Applying and demonstrating critical-thinking and creative-thinking skills in dance
- Making connections between dance and healthful living
- Making connections between dance and other disciplines

MATERIALS

- Music player with enough volume for the class space
- Music (CDs made from previous classes)
- Pencils for students who forget to bring them
- Paper clips to clip each group's Pathways Maps and Daily Contribution Sheets together, or use a folder for each group
- Projector and laptop
- One small music player for each project group (students may volunteer to bring these in if they are not available at school)
- Stopwatch for each group
- Workstation number signs
- Jazz Dance Project Rubric
- Bring a Pencil sign

PREPARATION

- Post Bring a Pencil sign.
- Have CDs of music that students chose for their group choreography. If two groups are using the same music, make two copies of the music or let groups work near each other with the same music player.
- Set up and space out music players for groups. Get extension cords if needed. If students bring in music players, label them with students' names and make provisions to store them safely.

- Laminate and post workstation number signs at music players.
- Set up projector and laptop to project handouts onto a wall (or have large posters made).

- Post stage directions and audience signs and Audience Etiquette sign if not previously posted.
- Mark off performance space with cones, tape, or flags (36 feet wide by 30 feet deep, or 11 by 9 m).

- Post outcomes for the lesson.

LESSON INTRODUCTION

When students enter the room, seat them in their warm-up spots facing the audience.

Review outcomes for the lesson.

WARM-UP

The warm-up is the same as in lesson 1.

➡ Today is the last day to work in your groups. At our next class, each group will perform their jazz dance. Notice the performance space. It is marked off with cones (or tape or flags). Today, groups will take turns coming to the performance space with their music player and practicing in the performance space. I'll call out the groups. Please move back and forth from your workstation to the performance space quickly so the groups can have as many turns as possible. One person from each group needs to pick up the Pathways Maps, Daily Contribution Sheets, and a stopwatch so you can time your group's dance. Go to your stations and complete your project. [Students do this.]

Note: As students work, circulate and note progress. If you think that an additional day of work would yield better results, or if students are working hard and are not finished, consider adding an extra day of group work. Remind students to complete Pathways Maps and Daily Contribution Sheets.

CLOSURE

Come over and have a seat with your group. One person from each group needs to collect the Pathways Maps, Daily Contribution Sheets, and stopwatch and turn them in.

➡ • **Option 1:** You have worked very hard for the past three days. The projects are complete. Tomorrow, we will watch each group perform their jazz dance. I'm excited to see what the groups have done. I saw some very creative and fun projects. Make sure you practice at home as well.

• **Option 2:** Each group has been working very hard, and it looks like everyone's project would benefit from having one more day (or two more days) to work and practice. [You can decide based on class length, attentiveness of students, and so on.] Make sure you practice at home as well.

• Did you meet your outcomes for today?

• Do you have any questions?

Note: If option 2 is chosen, repeat lesson 8.

9

JAZZ DANCE CHOREOGRAPHY PROJECT PERFORMANCE

OUTCOMES

- Students will exhibit appropriate audience etiquette.
- Students will perform their choreographed jazz dance.
- Students will evaluate pieces of choreography by using both the Jazz Dance Performance Self-Assessment and Jazz Dance Performance Group Assessment handouts.

NATIONAL DANCE STANDARDS

- Identifying and demonstrating movement elements and skills in performing dance
- Understanding choreographic principles, processes, and structures
- Understanding dance as a way to create and communicate meaning
- Applying and demonstrating critical-thinking and creative-thinking skills in dance
- Making connections between dance and healthful living
- Making connections between dance and other disciplines

MATERIALS

- Music player with enough volume for the class space
- Music (CDs made from previous classes)
- Pencils for students who forget to bring them
- Paper clips to clip each group's Pathways Maps and Daily Contribution Sheets together, or use a folder for each group
- Projector and laptop
- One small music player for each project group (students may volunteer to bring these in if they are not available at school)
- Stopwatch for each group

• Workstation number signs

• Bring a Pencil sign

• Jazz Dance Performance Self-Assessment, Jazz Dance Performance Group Assessment, Teacher's Assessment of Performance, and Critique Guidelines

PREPARATION

• Post outcomes for the lesson.

• Post Bring a Pencil sign.

• Have CDs of music that students chose for their group choreography. If two groups are using the same music, make two copies of the music or let groups work near each other with the same music player.

- Set up and space out music players for groups. Get extension cords if needed. If students bring in music players, label them with students' names and make provisions to store them safely.

- Laminate and post workstation number signs at music players.

- Set up projector and laptop to project handouts onto a wall (or have large posters made).

- Post stage directions and audience signs and Audience Etiquette sign.

- Mark off the performance space with cones, tape, or flags (about 36 feet wide by 30 feet deep, or 11 by 9 m).

- Run off enough copies of Jazz Dance Performance Self-Assessment, Jazz Dance Performance Group Assessment, and Critique Guidelines for all students. Put these on a table so students can pick them up on their way out of class.

- Run off enough copies of Teacher's Assessment of Jazz Dance Performance to assess each group.

LESSON INTRODUCTION

When students enter the room, seat them in their warm-up spots facing the audience.

Review the outcomes for the lesson.

WARM-UP

The warm-up is the same as in lesson 1.

Today we will perform our jazz dances. Before we do so, let's review how an audience responds to a performance. [Review audience etiquette and stress with students that this is part of their grade.]

Now you will have a short amount of time to run through your projects *once* with your music, and then the groups will perform. One person from each group should pick up the Pathways Map and Daily Contribution Sheets. Go to your stations for your run-through. [Students do this; allow about 15 minutes.]

Come to the audience area. One person in each group needs to turn in all group members' Pathways Maps and Daily Contribution Sheets. Everyone needs to have a seat in the center of the audience wall. [The wall that you have been using as the audience, or downstage, is the audience area where students sit with their backs to the wall, facing the stage.] Which group would like to go first? [In some classes, everyone will volunteer. In other classes, no one will volunteer. Have a designated order, draw numbers, or use some other method to determine performance order.] What is the etiquette for the audience? [Students respond with what has been posted.] Give group _____ your attention. [Start the music. You may want to count "5, 6, 7, 8" to help the group begin.]

At the end of each performance, insist that everyone applaud. Review audience etiquette, if necessary. Ask a question about each performance, such as these:

- What did you notice that was neat?

- What movement caught your eye?

• What was interesting about the group's performance?

• Did the group meet the requirements of the project?

• How do you know this?

Any other questions are fine, as long as they do not single out a particular student's performance.

CLOSURE

 You all did fabulous jazz dances and created movement that was fun to watch. What was most difficult about doing this project? [Students answer.] What did you enjoy most about the project? [Students answer.] To finish our unit, you are going to fill out the Jazz Dance Performance Self-Assessment, a Jazz Dance Performance Group Assessment, and a written critique of one group. The assessments and critique are homework. The assessments are due in the next class, and the critique is due on the date at the bottom of the Critique Guidelines sheet. The instructions for the critique are on the sheet. Your language arts teacher has gone over this in class. Be sure to meet the deadlines for each of these three assignments. Pick up these three sheets on your way out of class.

Note: If the language arts teacher was not able to review the guidelines, review them with students at this time.

EXTENSION

• If time for another lesson is available, videotape the performances and have students watch the videos before writing their critiques. This gives them a better opportunity to watch themselves performing.

• Use the projects for performance at events at the school or in the community.

• Add costumes, props, or sets.

• Combine several of the projects that are similar in style and have the students perform them one after the other with exits and entrances.

• Have the class vote on which project they would like to learn and have that group teach it to the class.

• If time permits, give each group a summary of the points made in the critiques of their performance. Add class periods to give groups time to incorporate some of the points made and perform their dance again. Part of this work should be for the group to write down why they decided to incorporate points or not and to explain this to the audience. Suggest adding this extension so that if students really get into it, they can have the experience of discussion and reworking choreography.

You Made It! Now What?

Students can go much further with these units with some enhancements. After teaching each lesson for the first time, make a list of what the students found easy and hard, what the students liked, what skills need more time, what performance qualities need work, and so on. Consider spending an extra day working on improving several of the skills, such as longer leaps in plyometrics. Or spend a day finding different ways to do skills the students liked, such as changing levels or adding turns or jumps.

DEVELOPING "EYES"

Take time to develop students' "eyes." For example, have half of the class or a small group do the warm-up while the rest watch. Ask students to look for correct technique and be able to tell specifically what they saw (for example, "Most of the students kept their feet parallel"). Students may not cite specific students! Also ask students to look for incorrect technique and specifically cite that as well (for example, "Some knees and toes were not facing the ceiling in the straddle"). This can be done with any segment of any lesson. Students with "eyes" are much better able to correct their own technique, which is crucial for success in any activity. In the same way, students can work with partners and coach one on one as a particular skill is performed, then change places—the coach becomes the performer.

COMMUNITY DANCE OPPORTUNITIES

Students may want to do more dancing. Find out what is offered in the community—from private lessons to municipal recreation classes. Be sure to include all styles of dance. Students can help with this. They may know that there is country line dancing at their church every Wednesday, or that there is a yoga class at the library on Tuesday, and so on.

Be sure not to show favoritism to any particular studio, style of dance, or organization. In other words, be all inclusive. Encourage students and parents to take class together. In our area, there is a tap class for kids and parents that is hugely popular—kid and parent must attend together.

COSTUMES AND PROPS

Students may want costumes and props for their projects. Set some criteria and encourage these enhancements, making sure they are safe (such as foam, not wooden, swords), secure, and appropriate for the ages of the students and the movement. Here are some suggestions for costumes:

- Do not allow bare midriffs.
- Dancers wearing leotards must also wear tights, leggings, or body stockings.

- Costumes may not shed (that is, no glitter) because material that gets on the floor becomes a cleaning issue and sticks to dancers' bare feet.
- Costumes must remain secure during dances (they must fit properly and not need adjusting).

STUDENT RESEARCH

It might become evident that students love a particular type of music used in class. Have students research that type of music and the artists who performed the genre. Using the Beatles as an example, students could report on how the group formed, their background, their big break, and the motivation for the songs they wrote. Grandparents, parents, and the Internet are good resources for this history lesson.

Students might want to know more about a particular step or skill. They can research the origin of the step and learn about the country, the person who created it, the reason for the name, the styles of dance that use the step, and more.

The possibilities are endless. You and your students can use your own curiosity as motivation to learn the details of any part of a lesson.

STUDENT-DIRECTED PROJECT

If time is available, students could work with different people in a new group and do another project that they created without a project card. This would mean having the students come up with the criteria for their projects and make a card for it including a name, assessment criteria, and so on. In other words, instead of having you direct the process for the project, students could direct the process from start to finish, and you could act as a resource if needed. You will need to stipulate a time line with benchmarks so that students use their time wisely and productively.

USING YOUR OWN CREATIVITY

We are all creative, even if we don't know it! Once the units have been taught, new criteria cards can be created based on the community. For example, when the community revolves around an industry, a card for that industry could be added as another project (an example is "On the Assembly Line" in Detroit). If the community is known for a sport, add a card such as "Surviving the Bobsled" in snow country. Create project cards based on cultures that the students are studying in other classes or on topics in science. The ideas are endless.

Be creative with your studio. Assign each student a vocabulary word from the unit and have them draw a picture that shows their word. Make a word wall of their art work. Take pictures of the students dancing. Have the students make a collage of their class and put the collage up on the wall. Look for posters of dancers (male and female). There are plenty in the various dance magazines. Laminate and place the posters around the studio.

Have each class create a class slogan relative to dance. Post their slogans. In this way, the students take ownership of their studio.

Knowing that something new will happen in each class creates excitement. Besides the skills, the music used could be the theme for the day (such as the 1950s). You could wear something typical of the genre. You can tell the students ahead of time to also wear something typical of the genre. In improvisation, the vocabulary for the day could be an activity. Students in small groups could, for example, spell the word forward and backward through their movement. Or they could improvise the definition of the word. Add the variables of body, energy, space, and time (BEST), and the possibilities are endless.

Students could begin doing these activities as soon as they enter the studio. The first five students are a group and begin. The next five are a group and begin, and so on. The word and aspect of BEST could be posted in a specific place so that students know where to look.

USING LIVE MUSIC

Talk with the music teacher to find out if there are students who can keep a good, consistent beat on drums. It is a good experience for the drummer to accompany the class and keep a steady tempo. It is also a good experience for dancers to move to live music and adjust if the tempo changes. This might take a little practice—the drummer must pick up the tempo that you set, and you need to be able to count out the desired tempo for the drummer.

SHOWCASING DANCE

Consider forming a dance performing group. The projects could be refined and performed for an assembly, as part of a talent show, at a school system dance festival, at a teachers' or principals' meeting, or for any community event (community fair, crafts show, talent show, area dance festival, mall performance). The performing group might create their own dances for specific events. The group could meet after school, at lunch, or whenever it is workable. It could be an honor for a project to be selected for the performing group. The more dance is showcased, the more effort will be made to keep the program, and the more students will be interested in taking dance in school and students and parents will be invested in the dance program.

INVOLVING PARENTS

Parents can be an asset. A parent–student group could rehearse and perform with the students. Dads could do an easy swing dance, jitterbug, or Broadway-style dance with their daughters. Moms could do the same with their sons. Dads and sons could do a Star Wars–type battle scene. Moms and daughters could do a pretty lyrical dance. Students will have all kinds of ideas.

Parents can be very helpful with organization, transportation, costumes, videography, photography, music, and much more. The key to channeling parent help is organizing their duties ahead of time and giving clear directions (in writing is best) for what is needed. Parents need to understand that all school policies and procedures must be followed and that you are the director.

ARTS SHOW

Start a talent show if the school does not have one. Involve all of the arts: chorus, band, orchestra, visual art, theater. Visual art could be hung for a gallery stroll to kick off the event, then you could have performances from various groups. If there is a sewing class in the school, students could design and make costumes as a class project. Students could write a skit in language arts and perform it in the show. The more students involved, the more parents will attend the event, and the more positive promotion of the arts program. You and other teachers could dance with the students!

SYSTEM-WIDE PROMOTION

If your school is the pilot for teaching the dance units, have the students write about what they learned during their experience. Make copies of the students' writing and have them available for the principal, guidance counselors, teachers in other schools who want to start the program, supervisors, and other personnel in the system who can advocate for dance.

If several schools in the district are teaching dance units, start a district dance day in which the schools come together and perform selected projects as a way of sharing what they have done (rather than a competition). A schedule of rehearsals in the performance space and perhaps classes in a specific style of dance could be part of the day. You can invite parents and others in the community to attend the performance. This could be done as a field trip or on a weekend depending on availability of substitutes or feasibility of students missing a day of school.

The more that dance can be positively shown to as many people as possible, the more support for the program will be gained. Annual dance events will become a part of the school and community. A budget may become available for the program. Support for taking students to a dance performance may occur. Teachers, students, and community will present ideas to enhance the program. Who knows where it might lead?

CONCLUSION

After having students ask for dance classes and using the minimal background I had from modern dance classes in college, visual art training in high school, and music lessons for 16 years, I realized that more was needed. I signed up for a jazz class thinking that would be the easiest. Wrong! It quickly became apparent that in order to be a good jazz dancer, I needed to study ballet, modern, and tap. After more than 20 years of classes in ballet, modern, jazz, tap, musical theater, yoga, Pilates, and as much cultural dance as I could get, I realized that dance is a wonderful way to stay fit, express emotions, free the soul, unload stress, and be creative. My roots go back to physical education, health, and competitive sports. That background combined with dance is amazing. I continue to take dance classes and work out, and it has become a way of life! Ideally, dance will have the same lasting benefits for your students—a lifelong extension.

Resources

WEB SITES

Dynamix Music: www.dynamixmusic.com.
Maryland Council for Dance: www.MarylandDance.org.
National Dance Association: www.aahperd.org/nda.
National Dance Education Organization: www.ndeo.org.

BOOKS

Alter, M. 1998. *Sport Stretch*. 2nd Ed. Champaign, IL: Human Kinetics.

Giordano, G. 1978. *Anthology of American Jazz Dance*. 2nd Ed. Evanston, IL: Orion.

Giordano, G. 1992. *Jazz Dance Class*. Pennington, NJ: Princeton Books.

Green Gilbert, A. 2006. *Brain Compatible Dance Education*. National Dance Association/AAHPERD.

Kassing, G. 2007. *History of Dance*. Champaign, IL: Human Kinetics.

Laws, K. 1984. *The Physics of Dance*. New York: Schirmer Books.

McGreevy-Nichols, S., H. Scheff, and M. Sprague. 2005. *Building Dances*. 2nd Ed. Champaign, IL: Human Kinetics.

McGreevy-Nichols, S. 2001. *Building More Dances*. Champaign, IL: Human Kinetics.

Sprague, M. 2006. *Dance About Anything*. Champaign, IL: Human Kinetics.

PUBLICATIONS

Arts Education Partnership. 2002. *Critical Links: Learning in the Arts and Student Academic and Social Development*. ISBN 1-884037-78-X. www.aep-arts.org.

National Dance Association. 1996. *National Standards for Dance Education*. ISBN 0-88314-750-5.

National Dance Education Organization. 2005. *Standards for Learning and Teaching Dance in the Arts: Ages 5-18*. www.ndeo.org.

Quigley, M., and J. Mehrhof. 2007. The impact of dance on high school athletes' agility and flexibility. *KAHPERD Journal 07*: 24-28.

MISCELLANEOUS

Action Based Learning. Jean Blaydes Madigan. www.actionbasedlearning.com.
Sound Machine portable sound systems. www.soundprojections.com.

ABOUT THE AUTHOR

Judi Fey, MEd, is the dance consultant for Anne Arundel County Public Schools in Annapolis, Maryland. She has taught dance over 30 years, founded and directed the South River Dance Company, and written K-12 dance curriculum for Anne Arundel County Public Schools and the Maryland State Department of Education. She has also organized numerous dance festivals, mentored and provided professional development to K-12 dance teachers, and taught the material in the book.

Fey is a member of the American Alliance for Health, Physical Education, Recreation and Dance (AAHPERD), the Maryland AHPERD, and the National Dance Education Organization. She has served terms as vice president, secretary, and treasurer of MAHPERD, and she has also served on the boards of the Maryland Council for Dance and the Ballet Theatre of Maryland. She was named Dance Teacher of the Year in 1989 by MAHPERD and was a national finalist for the AAHPERD Dance Teacher of the Year in 1999. She enjoys alpine skiing, travel, and dance-related classes in her leisure time.

DVD-ROM User Instructions

The PDFs on this DVD-ROM can only be accessed using a DVD-ROM drive in a computer (not a DVD player on a television). To access the PDFs, follow these instructions:

Microsoft Windows

1. Place DVD in the DVD-ROM drive of your computer.
2. Double-click on the My Computer icon from your desktop.
3. Right-click on the DVD-ROM drive and select the Open option from the pop-up menu.
4. Double-click on the Documents and Resources folder.
5. Select the PDF file that you want to view or print.

Macintosh

1. Place DVD in the DVD-ROM drive of your computer.
2. Double-click the DVD icon on your desktop.
3. Double-click on the Documents and Resources folder.
4. Select the PDF file that you want to view or print.

Note: You must have Adobe Acrobat Reader to view the PDF files.